SS-Panzer-Division *"Frundsberg"*

The 10th SS-Panzer-Division "Frundsberg"

Rolf Michaelis

Schiffer Military History
Atglen, PA

Book translation by Christine Wisowaty

Book Design by Ian Robertson.

Copyright © 2008 by Schiffer Publishing.
Library of Congress Control Number: 2008937585

Printed in China.
ISBN: 978-0-7643-3099-5

This book was originally published in German under the title
Die 10. SS-Panzer-Division "Frundsberg" by Michaelis-Verlag

We are interested in hearing from authors with book ideas on related topics.

Published by Schiffer Publishing Ltd.
4880 Lower Valley Road
Atglen, PA 19310
Phone: (610) 593-1777
FAX: (610) 593-2002
E-mail: Info@schifferbooks.com.
Visit our web site at: www.schifferbooks.com
Please write for a free catalog.
This book may be purchased from the publisher.
Please include $5.00 postage.
Try your bookstore first.

In Europe, Schiffer books are distributed by:
Bushwood Books
6 Marksbury Avenue
Kew Gardens
Surrey TW9 4JF, England
Phone: 44 (0) 20 8392-8585
FAX: 44 (0) 20 8392-9876
E-mail: Info@bushwoodbooks.co.uk.
Visit our website at: www.bushwoodbooks.co.uk
Free postage in the UK. Europe: air mail at cost.
Try your bookstore first.

Contents

Foreword

In August 2006 Literature Nobel Prize winner Günter Grass revealed that in 1944/45 he was a soldier of the *Waffen-SS*; more precisely, *Ladeschütze* in the 10. *SS-Panzer-Division* "Frundsberg." This surprising confession after 60 years put off the SPD (Social Democratic Party of Germany) author's supporters. With a heavy heart they were forced to leave behind fond collective judgments and general accusations. Suddenly, distinctions were being made between front soldiers and concentration camp henchmen. Grass himself stressed: "I was not involved in any criminal acts."

The "Frundsberger" may likely lay claim to the latter. Their unit, according to historian Bernd Wegner, was "militarily a good division." There were also no criminal accusations from the Allied side. Grass writes in his memoirs *Beim Häuten der Zwiebel* that he did not witness anything of a corrupt nature within his troop:

"I will have rather seen the *Waffen-SS* as an elite unit that was always deployed when a front invasion had to be sealed off, when a pocket, like the Demyansk pocket, had to be forced open, or Kharkiv had to be recaptured."

That was the prevailing view then. Also, after the war, *Bundeskanzler* Konrad Adenauer and opposition leader Kurt Schumacher stressed the military character of the *Waffen-SS* ("Soldier like any other"). Isolated war crimes, as they had occurred on all sides, should not damage the honor of the men, and their units, who remained respectable. The case of Grass led back to this fundamental realization.

Nevertheless, this by any means does not give cause to gloss over the terror and suffering of the war. Countless human tragedies and hecatombs of victims have been burned into the memory of the nations involved. Not least, the politicians in Berlin should consider this before they send German soldiers abroad—once again—to achieve their goals. The history of the *Division* "Frundsberg," documented here by Rolf Michaelis, by all means, urges peace.

Harald Neubauer
Member of the European Parliament 1989-1994

Deployment

In 1942 U.S. President Roosevelt promised Stalin the establishment of a second front in Western Europe for the relief of the Red Army. Without the prospect of a military success, on 19 August 1942 Operation "Jubilee" began—the landing of 5,000 British-Canadian soldiers at Dieppe. In contrast to Roosevelt, British Prime Minister Churchill believed that the time for invasion had not yet come. However, he agreed to the operation for propagandistic reasons! The attack of the 2nd Canadian Division under the command of Major General Roberts ultimately resembled self-sacrifice. Less than half of the deployed Allied soldiers arrived back in England. Nearly 1,200 had fallen, and approximately 1,600 were taken into German war captivity.

Hitler was aware of the potential danger in the west and, therefore, on 19 December 1942 ordered the formation of a central reserve in Normandy in the form of two new *SS* divisions (collective strength of approximately 40,000 men) in the region of the *Oberbefehlshaber* "West." It was to involve motorized units that, in the case of a large-scale Allied landing, were to annihilate the enemy troops on land by quick maneuvering. The OKW war journal documented the plans for the replacements:

"As directed by the Führer, *the order of securing of replacements for the formation of two new* SS *divisions until 1 February 1943 has been issued. For this purpose 27,000 men with the birth year of 1925 will be obtained through advertisements in RAD, 10,000 men from* Aktion Rü 43 Tausch *and 5,000 ethnic Germans; if the latter 15,000 can not be mustered, the birth year 1925 will have to produce a correspondingly higher number. The* Reichsarbeitsführer *asks for the cooperation with the advertisement of the birth year 1925.*

In order to spare this age group as much as possible, the Chief of Army Equipment and Commander of the Replacement Army received the order to commandeer those of younger age groups (24 and 23) to voluntary report to the SS; kv men, who until now were deemed unfit for the SS, will be taken on. Finally, 800 men who were pared down at the V.G.A.D. in autumn, will be placed at the disposal of the SS."

While there were disputes between the *Wehrmacht, Reichsarbeitsdienst*, and *Waffen-SS* regarding the conscription of the necessary recruits, the *SS-Führungshauptamt* (SS-FHA) had already on 8 January 1943 ordered the formation of staff for two *Panzer-Grenadier-Divisionen*.[1] The commander of the *SS-Junkerschule* Bad Tölz until now, *SS-Brigadeführer* and *Generalmajor der Waffen-SS* Lothar Debes,[2] was appointed commander of the formation, initially named *SS-Panzer-Grenadier-Division* 10.

---

1 SS-FHA, Kdo. Amt der Waffen-SS, Org. Tgb. Nr. 35/43 g. Kdos. from 8 January 1943.

Because the number from the *Reichsarbeitsdienst* of 27,000 volunteers could not be reached, the planned conscription for April/May 1943 of members of strategic trade and industry was pushed and increased to 20,000.

Assembly area of the *SS-Panzer-Grenadier-Division* 10 "Karl der Große"
February – July 1943

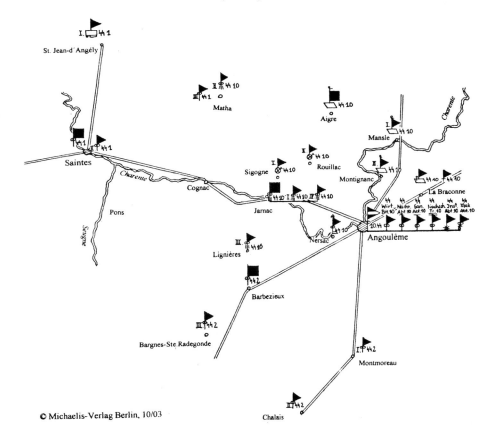

2 See appendix 7

As of February 1943 the recruits met in an 80 x 80 km large assembly area of the *SS-Panzer-Grenadier-Division* 10 in the region between Bordeaux – Limoges – La Rochelle in the region of the 1. *Armee*. The *Aufstellungsstäbe* were accommodated in the following quarters:

Divisionsstab	Angouléme
SS-Panzer-Grenadier-Regiment 1	Saintes
SS-Panzer-Grenadier-Regiment 2	Barbezieux
SS-Kradschützen-Regiment 10	Rouillac
SS-Panzer-Regiment 10	Aigre
SS-Panzerjäger-Abteilung 10	La Braconne
SS-Sturmgeschütz-Abteilung 10	La Braconne
SS-Artillerie-Regiment 10	Jarnac
SS-Flak-Abteilung 10	Angouléme
SS-Pionier-Bataillon 10	Nersac
SS-Nachrichten-Abteilung 10	Angouléme
SS-Sanitäts-Abteilung 10	Angouléme
SS-Wirtschafts-Bataillon 10	Angouléme
SS-Nachschub-Truppen 10	Angouléme
SS-Instandsetzungs-Abteilung 10	Angouléme

The formation of the *Panzer-Regiment* was delayed considerably due to the lack of vehicles. Only the II. *Abteilung*, which was equipped with Panzer IV, could be formed. Because these gradually became available, a "Panzer" *Abteilung* was to be formed with 42 *Sturmgeschütze* and three *Panzerbefehlswagen* (Panzer III) as an interim formation.[3] At its disbandment at the turn of the year 1943/44 the majority of the men, as well as the guns, came to *SS-Panzer-Regiment* 10.

On 1 March 1943 the division temporarily received the name
"Karl der Große."[4]
Hitler commented to the Kaiser as follows:[5]

"1200 years have passed since the birth of the man who, according to historical facts, to a great extent, in hard, bloody combat combined German tribes into one powerful empire for the first time:

---

3 OB "West," Tgb. Nr. III/35355 geh. from 24 June 1943
4 Karl der Große (Charlemagne) was born on 2 April 742 and as of 768 was King of the Francs. In 773/774 he conquered the Lombard Kingdom and conquered and Christianized the Saxons in multiple campaigns (772-804). In 788 Bavaria was incorporated into the Franconian Kingdom – in 795/796 the conquest of the Avar Kingdom followed. In 800 Pope Leo II appointed Karl der Große Roman Emperor. In over 30 years of combat he succeeded in increasing the borders of the Kingdom of the Franks so much, that it became the most significant empire of the western Middle Ages. In all educational and cultural works his severity was feared. In Verden alone in 782 he had 4,500 hostages executed in a single act.
5 Compare Dr. Picker, Henry: Hitlers Tischgespräche im Führerhauptquartier, Stuttgart 1976

Karl der Große. Also, our latest historical writings have not completely grasped the sense of this process. Severity must be used in order to be able to create toughness. What meant a loss of the most valuable traditions for many then was largely the formation of a state body, that alone was suited to build up resistance against the enemy, that constantly presses from the east and threatens. Only this first great formation of a German state can restore Austria in the south and thus establish a partition against the constant invasions of these strange tribes.

Since then we have also had to witness this same process from within, when finally the old Reich fell apart and shattered, disintegrated into a battle not only of dynasties but also finally between religious denominations."

The naming in itself was interesting: in 1935 Heinrich Himmler had the so-called Saxon Grove erected at Verden on the Aller—a memorial for the presumed approximately 4,500 Saxons murdered by Karl der Große in 782 AD (sic!). Several years later a *SS* division received its name! Hitler's ideas were certainly the decisive factor here, whereby Karl der Große was held in especially high esteem, primarily in France (here Charlemagne) as King of the Franks! Thus, the naming was to serve as propaganda in France; at the same time the formation of a French troop of the *Waffen-SS* was being urged. This later received the name "Charlemagne."

On 21 March 1943 the KTB/OKW documented the following on the existing conflicts between the *Wehrmacht* and the *Waffen-SS* with the new formation:

"Because the Reichsarbeitsführer *requested a central governance of the advertisements in RAD through the OKW, on 15 March the involved authorities of the OKW,* Wehrmacht *sections and RAD met for a discussion in which an agreement was made for an adequate plan.*

On 17 March the WFSt. established its basic stance, which was already expressed previously, that the volunteer system of the Waffen-SS *can no longer ensure their replacement need and, strength-wise, also harms the* Führer *and* Unterführer *recruits to a great extent. Therefore, a fundamental solution is urgent. First, the speech from the chief of the* Generalstab des Heeres *must be awaited.*

On 18 March in accordance with the Reichsarbeitsführer *regarding the basis of the plan from 15 March, the OKW issued a decree for advertising in RAD. The Chief OKW informed the Chief of the HPA, during his speech on the replacement situation it was reported to the* Führer *that the high number of volunteers (*Kriegsmarine *30,000,* Luftwaffe *35,000,* Waffen-SS *60,000, together 125,000) could not be maintained without repercussions on the* Führer *and especially the* Unterführer *recruits of the army. A change for the age-group 1925 is no longer possible.*

Arrival of the *Sturmgeschütze III* in France
1943.

Recruit of the *SS-Sturmgeschütz-Abteilung*
10.

The approved quota of the Waffen-SS *for the age-group 1926 (15,000 men) is expected to be increased. In the RAD from now on anticipation is out of the question, as the* Reichsarbeitsführer *would also like to enforce the decree from 18 March on the* Waffen-SS."*

The new formation of a division in this time of war always gave rise to numerous problems: in addition to the difficulties in materializing heavy weapons and equipment, the necessary, motivated training personnel were also lacking. *SS-Brigadeführer* and *Generalmajor der Waffen-SS* Debes issued a circular on 8 May 1943 to the commanders to counter the grievances that had arisen. It is notable that Debes addressed his *Führer* with "gentlemen," which was very unusual in the *Waffen-SS* (sic!):

"Because in many cases Führer, Unterfüher *and men did not display the proper conduct as it naturally must be for members of the division, I feel urged to request the gentlemen commanders, to work more than ever toward discipline as well as respectable behavior in and outside of service.*

Because more time for training is available due to the delay of motorization, as of Monday, 10 May 1943, one hour of exercises is to be incorporated into daily activities. Salutes are to be correspondingly practiced. The salute is the calling card of a troop.

It has also occurred to me numerous times that men have put on their belts poorly. Then it became apparent that for the most part the belts were too big and could not be buckled any tighter. Occasionally the proper fit of articles of clothing is left to be desired. Also, individual men are still wearing the Totenkopf *on their collar instead of the Sig Rune. From now on all units must hold uniform inspections and suppress complaints.*

Unterführer *and men must be informed that it is not at the individual's will whether or not he wears the collar of his coat open or closed. For the time being everyone must wear their collar closed. When the weather becomes warmer, the* Regiments-Kommandeur *or the commander of independent battalions, respectively, of independent detachments may permit the collar being worn open.*

The Führer *must wear the epaulet with the required branch of service colors.* Verwaltungsführer, *technical* Führer, *etc. wear the required epaulet. The necessary changes are to be carried out by 1 June 1943. The discipline of the guard leaves a lot to be desired. Recently I found out that an entire guard looked out of the window and observed the road traffic. A series of traffic accidents has made it necessary to point out the required driving discipline. I have judged the motor accidents that have occurred up until now relatively mildly, but have personally seen careless driving in the meantime. Corresponding instructions are to follow.*

Recently there was a motorcycle accident, during which the driver had severe internal injuries and died as a result. The SDG called in immediately after the accident had neither notified the doctor, nor took care of the continued transport of the victim effectively. On

France 1943

my order he was placed before a court martial. Although the investigation of this incident has not been finalized on all points, in the failure of the concerned SDG-Hauptscharführer *there is certainly a great neglect in his obligations.*

Despite my previous warning, alcoholic excesses have occurred. In one case three Unterscharführer *of the division were each sentenced to three months imprisonment. In a second case one* Unterscharführer *and 1* Sturmmann *each received two months imprisonment, and one* Rottenführer, *as well as one* Sturmmann *were sentenced to six weeks. In addition, the* Unterscharführer *was reduced in rank. In a third case that is still pending, I had a* Führer *arrested and taken to the* Abteilung für Offiziere der Kriegs-Wehrmachts-Haftanstalt *Cognac. The* Führer *concerned faced his court-martialled sentence. As an SS man, one does not use spare money for alcoholic excess, but rather offers it to the winter relief.*

The cases I presented have caused me to advise the commanders of their supervisory responsibilities."

The personnel strength of the division grew astonishingly quickly. For the 10.*SS-Panzer-Grenadier-Division* "Karl der Große" the KTB/OKW reported the following strength:

4 April 1943	13,787 men
10 April 1943	13,882 men
13 April 1943	14,171 men
15 April 1943	14,597 men
24 April 1943	16,323 men
27 April 1943	17,657 men
12 May 1943	18,625 men
27 May 1943	18,810 men
5 June 1943	18,846 men
11 June 1943	19,138 men

With this, the *SS* unit had a significantly higher strength of enlisted personnel at their disposal than a *Panzer-Grenadier-Division* of the army. This can be explained by the fact that Himmler initially wanted to create potential for replacements to the *Stammdivisionen* or further new formations of the *Waffen-SS*.

Because the German wartime economy was not in a position to meet all requirements, in June 1943 a new motor vehicle requirement for all "*Kriegsstärkenachweisungen*" (KStN) was determined by the *Organisations-Stab z. b. V.* in the OKW. According to this, with new formations and replenishment 75% of the prior requirement should be allocated. However, this only documented what was factual in practice– for the most part, these units

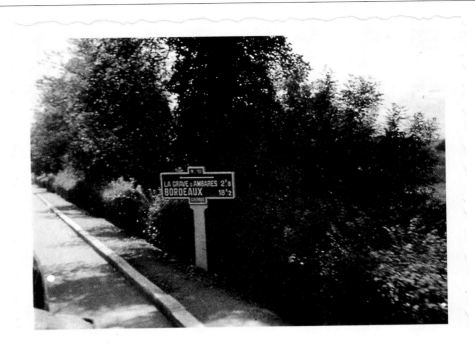

Assembly area of the 10. *SS-Panzer-Grenadier-Division* in the Bordeaux region.

Bordeaux

Bordeaux - port

Bayonne July 1943 – Quarters of the *SS-Flak-Abteilung* 10.

did not once reach 50% of the requirement. Also, the equipment of all Western divisions with heavy anti-tank guns was limited to 21. The Paks thereby freed were provided to the 65., 284., and 715. *Infanterie-Division*.

In July 1943 the 10. *SS-Panzer-Grenadier-Division* transferred to an 80 x 80 km large region east of Biarritz. The *SS-Kradschützen-Regiment*—partly referred to as a "quick regiment"—was disbanded, and from this a *SS-Panzer-Aufklärungs-Abteilung* was formed.

Quarters of the 10. *SS-Panzer-Grenadier-Division* July/August 1943

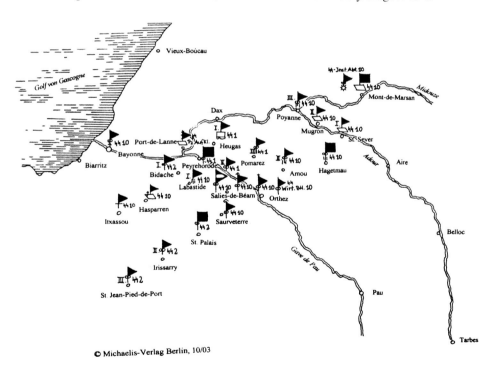

The units took up quarters in the following towns:

Divisionsstab	Salies-de-Béarn
SS-Panzer-Grenadier-Regiment 1	Peyrehorade
SS-Panzer-Grenadier-Regiment 2	St. Palais
SS-Panzer-Aufklärungs-Abteilung 10	Port-de-Lanne
SS-Panzer-Regiment 10	Mont-de-Marsan
SS-Panzerjäger-Abteilung 10	Itxassou
SS-Sturmgeschütz-Abteilung 10	Hasparren
SS-Artillerie-Regiment 10	Hagetmau
SS-Flak-Abteilung 10	Bayonne
SS-Pionier-Bataillon 10	Sauveterre-de-Béarn
SS-Nachrichten-Abteilung 10	Salies-de-Béarn
SS-Sanitäts-Abteilung 10	Orthez
SS-Wirtschafts-Bataillon 10	Orthez
SS-Nachschub-Truppen 10	Puyoô
SS-Instandsetzungs-Abteilung 10	Mont-de-Marsan
SS-Pz. Gren. Ausb. u. Ers. Abt. 10[6]	Brünn

In late summer 1943 Italy's departure from the Axis Alliance with Germany was on the horizon. Hitler took precautions and transferred numerous units to the border area; more precisely, the regions occupied by Italian troops (primarily France and the Balkans). On 2 August 1943 the OKW informed the OB "West" that the 10. *SS-Panzer-Grenadier-Division* was being deployed for Operation "Siegfried," the takeover of the Southern French coast from the Italian 4ᵗʰ Army, and requested a report on the readiness for transport. The next day the KTB/OKW reported:

"*the 10.* SS-Panzer-Grenadier-Division *is likewise ready for transport… however, can depart on 7 August at the earliest and arrive in the Marseilles region on 9 – 13 August.*"

On 7 August 1943 the KTB/OKW reported:

"*The OKW informed the OB West that the* Führer *approved the requested stay of the 376. and 389. Div. on 4 August on the northern front (a misleading description, because the units were situated in the Netherlands, respectively northern France). For this, the 10.* SS-Panzer-Grenadier-Division *should be transported to the* Armeegruppe *Felber.*"

---

6 The *SS-Panzer-Grenadier-Ausbildungs- und Ersatz-Bataillon* 10 was formed on 1 May 1943 in Brünn from the previous *SS-Panzer-Grenadier-Ersatz-Bataillon* III (*SS-Panzer-Grenadier-Division* "Totenkopf"). Sections of the battalion were deployed during the Slovakian national uprising within the framework of the *SS-Panzer-Grenadier-Regiment* "Schill." In April 1945 the unit received the military postal service number 64 438 and was supplied to the 32. *SS-Freiwilligen-Grenadier-Division* " 30. Januar" on the Oder front. In the following battles the battalion had over 400 missing!

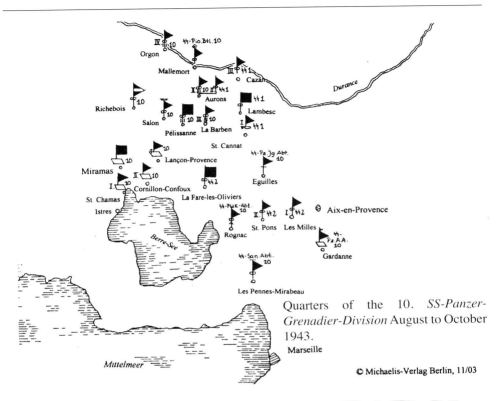

Quarters of the 10. *SS-Panzer-Grenadier-Division* August to October 1943.

© Michaelis-Verlag Berlin, 11/03

Summer 1943 in the Biarritz region.

The famous Bad Biarritz.

As of 10/11 August 1943 the division was transported through Pau-Toulouse-Narbonne via rail transport of the *Armeegruppe* "Felber" (as of 26 August 1943 19. *Armee*) to the region north of Marseilles, and the units were accommodated in the following locations (Quarters approximately 50 x 60 km):

Divisionsstab	Richebois
SS-Panzer-Grenadier-Regiment 1	Lambesc
SS-Panzer-Grenadier-Regiment 2	La Fare-les-Oliviers
SS-Panzer-Aufklärungs-Abteilung 10	Gardanne
SS-Panzer-Regiment 10	Miramas
SS-Panzerjäger-Abteilung 10	Eguilles
SS-Sturmgeschütz-Abteilung 10	Lançon-Provence
SS-Artillerie-Regiment 10	Pélissanne
SS-Flak-Abteilung 10	Rognac
SS-Pionier-Bataillon 10	Mallemort
SS-Nachrichten-Abteilung 10	Richebois
SS-Sanitäts-Abteilung 10	Les Pennes-Mirabeau
SS-Nachschub-Truppen 10	Salon-de-Provence

In Southern France training continued during the following weeks, and it was attempted to bring the equipment of the unit to its required strength. On 17 August 1943 the *Oberbefehlshaber* "West" announced the allocation of motor vehicles to both *SS-Panzer-Grenadier-Verbände*. In reality, all arriving vehicles were transferred to the 9. *SS-Panzer-Grenadier-Division* "Hohenstaufen."[7] Initially, nothing changed with the precarious equipment situation of the 10. *SS-Panzer-Grenadier-Division* "Frundsberg." Only after the extensive disarmament of the Italian Army in September 1943 (Italy's armistice with the Allies) by German troops could the equipment lacking be procured. On 11 October 1943 the KTB/OKW responded:

"*The* Generalstab des Heeres *is to immediately equip the 25.* Panzer-Division, *the* Panzer-Grenadier-Division *'Feldherrnhalle,' the 9. and 10.* SS-Panzer-Grenadier-Division *with Italian or other motor vehicles (as replacements of the motor vehicles provided to the 14.* Panzer-Division), *in order to mobilize the motorized units remaining in the west as quickly as possible.*"

A former member recalls:

"*In Summer 1942* Unterführer *of the* Waffen-SS *in* RAD-Lager Budweis K/1/384 *volunteered for enlistment into this troop. I reported…*

In late autumn the enlisting order to the Panzer-Pionier-Ersatz- und Ausbildungsbataillon *29 in Hann. Munden arrived. Training in water rescue and bridge building followed in this unit.*

---

7 OB West, Tgb. Nr. III/37347 geh. from 17 August 1943.

On 19 January 1943 three comrades and I received a marching order to the SS-Ausbildungs-Regiment *Prague. I remained here for approximately four weeks for basic training. In February 1943 I was detached to Pikovice and had to report to the 8. Kompanie.*

At the beginning of March 1943 we were transferred to France as SS-Panzer-Pionier-Kompanie *10. The journey led through Bar le duc – Angouleme to Lux near Mansle where the* SS-Panzer-Regiment *10 was situated.*

Lux is located close to the Charente, which a large bridge spanned. The terrain was partially swampy, everything was available to ensure proper training. SS-Obersturmführer *Brand was a hard* 'Soldatenmacher.' *Offenses were severely punished – a young combat engineer was sentenced to six months imprisonment for rabbit theft – I never saw the comrade again.*

The training was especially designed for mine clearing, Stoßtruppe *training with live ammunition. Goose step and rifle positioning were also included. The company had a motor vehicle, an old English passenger car, at its disposal. It was mostly in the workshop. In August 1943 we transferred to the Pau region. Shortly thereafter we were transported by rail through Monte Marsan to Miramas at St. Chamas. We moved into massive barracks here, where there was previously a* Wehrmacht *unit. It was teeming with flies. We earned our bread with field exercises and makeshift bridge construction. Excursions to Arles and Nimes were a nice change of pace. The makeshift bridges were given over to the village inhabitants, who gave thanks with roasts and wine at the village square. We generally had a good relationship with the population."*

Heinrich Himmler mentioned the formation of the 9. and 10. *SS-Division* in his speech on 4 October 1943 at the *SS-Gruppenführer* conference in Posen (today Poznan, in Poland). The plans for the formation of numerous new corps are interesting. The addressed *Generalkommando* VII. *SS-Panzer-Korps* was formed as of October 1943 with *SS-Gruppenführer* and *Generalleutnant der Waffen-SS* Kleinheisterkamp as commanding general, but was soon renamed *Generalkommando* IV. *SS-Panzer-Korps.* The 9. and 10. *SS-Division* were subsequently to report to the II. *SS-Panzer-Korps*:

"Since we last saw each other, we have advanced to the next stage of organizational development in the Waffen-SS. *1 ½ years ago, we were at the formation of the I. SS-Panzer-Korps that* SS-Obergruppenführer *Hausser led, who at this time is leading the operations in Italy at the littoral. In the meantime the following corps have emerged or are in formation:*

…The IV. SS-Panzer-Korps *under* SS-Gruppenführer *Krüger, who until now led the Division 'Das Reich,' consisting of two new divisions, namely the established* SS-Panzer-Division *'Hohenstaufen,' that we had mustered in February of the same year in the course of 5 to 6 weeks Berger as the 9. and 10. Division with* SS-Obergruppenführer, *and that we had trained and formed with* SS-Obergruppenführer *Jüttner.*

I can tell you, that was a feat, the greatest risk. It was the greatest state of anxiety that I felt for several weeks. The old Panzer-Korps, *existing of 'Reich,' 'Leibstandarte' and 'Totenkopf' came away from France. In the second half of December the order came from the* Führer: *On 15 February 1943 two new* SS *divisions will be in France, mustered from the 1925 age-group in the labor service camp. One could write a book about this later and recount how difficult it was and how it was deflected. From the first day these recruits shot with live ammunition because no one ever knew if the English were coming. After 8 weeks it was already significantly better, and now they have become outstanding divisions.*

Currently we have the assignment to form the 16. and 17. SS-Division until January. With this hard work we are all together busy. The IV. SS-Panzer-Korps will consist of the SS-Panzer-Division 'Hohenstaufen' (9. SS-Division) and of a division that is to be newly formed that will receive the name SS-Panzer-Grenadier-Division 'Reichsführer-SS.' *It will be formed from the* Brigade 'Reichsführer-SS' *that we hope came off well today with the last man from Corsica.*

…The VII. SS-Panzer-Korps, that being formed with an already existing SS-Panzer-Division (the 10. SS-Division) located in France, which received the name 'Frundsberg,' and the (17.) SS-Panzer-Grenadier-Division that initially received a strange-sounding, but – if understood correctly – very defiant name: 'Götz von Berlichingen.' 'Frundsberg' and 'Götz von Berlichingen,' that is a declaration of defiance from us to our opponents within and without."

A few days after Himmler's speech the 10. *SS-Panzer-Grenadier-Division* received the order to detail a battalion to the 2. *SS-Panzer-Grenadier-Division* "Das Reich" in Russia. They pulled back at the Dnieper at Krementschug (today Kremenchuk in the Ukraine), and marched toward the Shitomir (today Zhytomyr in the Ukraine) region at the beginning of November 1943. While the majority of the 2. *SS-Panzer-Grenadier-Division* "Das Reich" was detached from the front in mid-December and transferred to East Prussia to the Stablack military training area, the II./*SS-Panzer-Grenadier-Regiment* 2 joined the 10. *SS-Panzer-Grenadier-Division* within the framework of the *SS-Panzer-Kampfgruppe* "Das Reich." A former member recalls:

"On 19 October 1943 the Marsch-Bataillon *boarded the train and was unloaded in Debica at the end of October / beginning of November 1943. We were equipped thus far with only small arms – here we received heavy weapons, equipment and winter clothing. On 19 November 1943 we finally reached Berdischew in the Ukraine and were greeted by the commander of the* SS-Panzer-Grenadier-Regiment 4 "Der Führer" *and incorporated as II.* Bataillon. *The front assignment east of Shitomir followed…"*

Members of the *SS-Pionier-Bataillon* 10 in France 1943.

Training on the I. F. H. 10.5 cm (above) and s. F. H. 15 cm (below).

Panzer III — commanding tank of the *SS-Panzer-Artillerie-Regiment* 10.

On 26 October 1943 the SS-FHA announced Hitler's order to reorganize the division into a *Panzer-Division* and rename it to[8]

10. *SS-Panzer-Division* "Frundsberg."[9]

It came to be renamed because the French *Waffen-Verband* of the *SS* that was already in formation was to be named "Charlemagne" (Karl der Große)! At the same time, the unit—whose *Panzer-Grenadier-Regimenter* from now on bore the consecutive numbers 21 and 22—was transferred to northern France again and occupied the following quarters:

Divisionsstab	Lisieux
SS-Panzer-Grenadier-Regiment 21	le Pin
SS-Panzer-Grenadier-Regiment 22	N-D. d'Estrée
SS-Panzer-Regiment 10	Brionne
SS-Panzerjäger-Abteilung 10	Broglie
SS-Panzer-Aufklärungs-Abteilung 10	Orbec
SS-Panzer-Artillerie-Regiment 10	St. Pierre s/Dives
SS-Flak-Abteilung 10	Bernay
SS-Panzer-Pionier-Bataillon 10	Beuzeville
SS-Panzer-Nachrichten-Abteilung 10	Lisieux
SS-Sanitäts-Abteilung 10	Prêtreville
SS-Wirtschafts-Bataillon 10	Lisieux
SS-Divisions-Nachschubtruppen 10	Vimoutiers
SS-Feld-Ersatz-Bataillon 10	Lisieux

In an order of the day at the beginning of November 1943 *SS-Brigadeführer* Debes explained the new division's name "Frundsberg" to the men:

"The figure of Frundsberg has vanished from today's historical consciousness of the German people to a large extent. Besides his name and the fact that he was a German Landsknechtsführer, *few Germans know who Frundsberg was. As the* Führer *has given our division the name*

F r u n d s b e r g

This undeserved oblivion should be torn away. Frundsberg's unfailing commitment to the Reich and German affairs, the powerful, combative character of this man shall be reborn. For generations the Landsknecht *was the epitome of the original and superior soldierly power of our people.*

---

8 SS-FHA, Kdo. Amt der Waffen-SS, Org. Tgb. Nr. 1632/43 g. Kdos. from 26 October 1943.

9 Georg von Frundsberg was born on 24 September 1473 at Schloss Mindelheim in Memmingen. In 1499 he served under Kaiser Maximilian I. against Switzerland and was appointed knight in 1504. Frundsberg primarily led the *Söldnertruppe* known as *Landsknechte* and in 1513 went to war against Venice and in 1519 Ullrich von Württemberg. On 20 August 1528 Frundsberg died at the age of barely 55.

Although he may have been spoken ill of, in the name of Frundsberg his best strengths symbolically unite.

We shall bear the name of this great German with pride! Frundsberg is a model in this battle that we must lead for the people and the Reich!

It must be our sacred will to live up to this proud name."

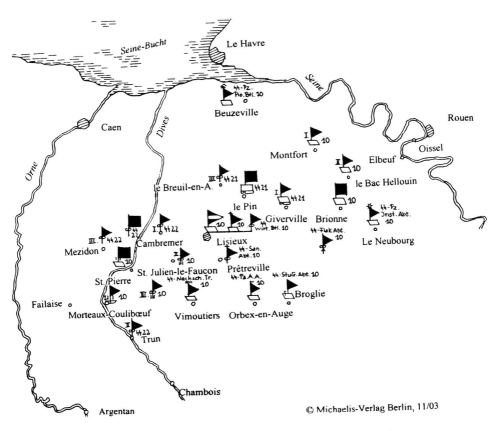

Quarters of the 10. *SS-Panzer-Division* "Frundsberg"
November 1943 – March 1944

In autumn 1943 *SS-Brigadeführer* Debes (2ⁿᵈ from the left) handed over the 10. *SS-Panzer-Division* "Frundsberg" to *SS-Brigadeführer* von Treuenfeld (2ⁿᵈ from the right)

Lothar Debes at a veterans' reunion in 1955.

In the course of the reorganization into a *Panzer-Division* the unit also received a new required strength. Because this was approximately 1,500 men less than the actual strength, the surplus men were used for new formations of the *Waffen-SS*. On 12 November 1943 the KTB/OKW noted:

"*The OKW agrees with the transfer and relocation of the released sections of the 9. and 10.* SS-Panzer-Division *that are meant for the formation of the 17. and 16.* SS-Panzer-Grenadier-Division."

Among others, both 15. (*Kradschützen*) *Kompanien* of the *SS-Panzer-Grenadier-Regimenter* 21 and 22 were transferred for the formation of the *SS-Panzer-Aufklärungs-Abteilung* 17, as well as the III./*SS-Panzer-Artillerie-Abteilung* 10 for *Artillerie-Regiment* of the 17. *SS-Panzer-Grenadier-Division* "Götz von Berlichingen."

On 15 November 1943 the previous *Befehlshaber der Waffen-SS* "Russland-Süd," *SS-Brigadeführer* and *Generalmajor der Waffen-SS* von Treuenfeld,[10] took over the 10. *SS-Panzer-Division* "Frundsberg." SS-*Gruppenführer* and *Generalleutnant der Waffen-SS* Debes was assigned with the command of the 6. *SS-Gebirgs-Division* "Nord" in Karelia. *SS-Brigadeführer* von Treuenfeld, who was rather suited as political agitator than commander of a combat unit, gave instructions on 25 November 1943 for the ideological training of the division:

"*Through talks on the greatest epochs of German history, the pride to be part of the German people should be awoken in each man. He does not need to know the details, it is sufficient for him as a result of the education that...in all of the centuries of the German past there were battles against enemies from within and without until the* Führer *was able to achieve a great unification of all Germans. He must know that it is up to each of us how the* Führer *will shape the future of the Reich.*

Through talks on our opponents each man should be bred to be a fanatical hater... It does not matter to which front our division will be deployed: the unruly hate of the opponent, no matter if he is an Englander, American, Jew or Bolshevik, must empower each of our men to ultimate deeds."

The upheaval in Italy in late summer 1943 had led to numerous troops being pulled out of France, as well. While the 10. *SS-Panzer-Division* "Frundsberg" remained in France, the 9. *SS-Panzer-Division* received the order on 8 February 1944 to be constantly ready for transfer. In this respect, the still present lack of weapons and equipment was to be taken over by the 10. *SS-Panzer-Division*. Because a potential transfer of the 9. *SS-Panzer-Division* to Italy was soon abandoned, the 10. *SS-Panzer-Division* did also not need to hand over any equipment.

---

10 See Appendix 7

In fact, the first deployment was imminent—the one-year training ended. The commander of the *SS-Panzer-Regiment* 10, *SS-Obersturmbannführer* Kleffner, wrote on 15 January 1944 in his regiment's order of the day concerning this:

"Proudly we look at our Panzer-Regiment, *that today is celebrating its one year existence.*

We have experienced many hard, but many nice hours together this year. From a mass of people we have formed one company after the other in untiring effort and raised the members to soldiers. As long as we had no tanks, we had trained as infantrymen, we have familiarized ourselves with warfare of the Panzerwaffe *in sandbox exercises, map exercises, etc. We have gained a rich knowledge and ability with various courses that offer us the foundation for a promising mission.*

I thank all the Führer, Unterführer *and men for their model groundwork on our regiment.*

I expect that in time, each who is available for our mission refines himself in order to become a 100 percent, full-fledged Panzermann.

The fate of the Reich, and with this the groundwork of the Führer, *lies in the hands of the* Panzerwaffe. *In the old spirit of the* Panzerwaffe

'Vorwärts-Ran!'

In this year we want to do more than duty demands of us.

Long live the Führer! *Long live Germany!"*

A former member of the *SS-Pionier-Bataillon* 10 recalls the formation of the battalion:

"Pionierschule of the Waffen-SS *in Hradischko, beginning of January 1943. For the first time the candidates for* Führer *for the new* Pionier-Bataillon met. SS-Hauptsturmführer *Wendler became commander. We looked at each other and thought that we fit together well. The companies were formed. Service began, weapons training, 'Sperrdienst,' driving school. One day the following incident occurred:*

After a visit from Inspektion 5 all Führer *of the battalion, except* SS-Hauptsturmführer *Wendler, were ordered into a lecture hall. Seats were spread out like during a test and the* Führer *of the school supervised. An uneasy atmosphere spread. A series of questions that concerned our commander and our* Führer *were presented to us for written answers. Finally we were informed that questions were pointless, visiting Prague off-duty was not permitted, and inquiries of Wendler were explicitly forbidden.*

That was a shock for us. In some ways it seemed possible to me to find our good Wendler in a small psychopathic ward in Prague around midnight. These instances brought about a deep suspicion in us.

SS-Hauptsturmführer *Benz was suggested as the successor of the commander, with him the battalion then transferred to France in April.* SS-Hauptsturmführer *Wendler departed from us at the train and promised to follow soon. We were unloaded north of Angouleme and moved into cantonment on both sides of the Charante. The population behaved decently– we were not the first German soldiers here.*

Stoßtrupp *training was practiced emphatically and closing company training with armed weapons gave the command and men confidence and security. Unfortunately, at the conclusion of a company exercise there were critical remarks before the assembled company by the commander that provoked protest and internal aggression. After unrefined remarks were said at lunch at the* Führer *table, there was a written complaint by the division that resulted in the replacement of* SS-Hauptsturmführer *Benz and* SS-Obersturmführer *Hermann. This whole matter was blamed on the entire battalion and continued to affect everyone adversely. After leaving the command of the 1.* Armee *and being supplied to the 15.* Armee, *the* SS-Pionier-Bataillon *10 was also transferred to the southwest and moved into cantonment south of Pau and into blocking sectors in the western section of the Pyrenees. However, before the blocking objects (railway tunnel and passes to Spain) could be further developed with mines and explosives, the transfer of the division to the Mediterranean region took place. The* SS-Pionier-Bataillon *10 moved into quarters north of Aix – the new commander was* SS-Hauptsturmführer *Tröbinger. Within a larger scope, the units carried out alarm and marching exercises in a motorized unit, lorried or on foot. In the last week of October the division was transferred back to Normandy.*

One night during the transport jesting words were flying back and forth in the compartment if anyone had not forgotten to make their will over the skat game… I wanted to protest because of these comments, but a giant fist stopped the train, the doors sprung open, as if by magic, the luggage was pulled down and the people were confused. Then the train tore forward, again this powerful braking, and outside commotion and eerie hissing. A Signaltrupp *was sent to the back because other trains followed us. As I went forward the first mutilated dead of the 2.* Kompanie *were brought into tent squares. The young* Kompanieführer *was completely desperate, he brought two Frenchman in front of him and had the MPi ready to shoot. I was only barely able to stop him from his plan. It concerned two shift workers of the French railway.*

The locomotive was half on its side, bored itself between both tracks up to half the boiler, steam streamed out of the torn pipes, and the blaze shot out of the fire hole. The first three all-terrain vehicles had piled up high and plowed into each other, in the system of rods the camouflage jackets could be recognized. In another all-terrain vehicle there was still life, but we were hardly able to help. I then saw that the tracks were detached on a bridge. A kind fate prevented them from being transferred out… Not until the morning hours did the Bauzug *arrive with special equipment. Our transport train was repositioned and later ran on the neighboring track into Normandy, was unloaded in Pont Audemer and moved into quarters in the region west and southwest.*

In November/December 1943 the battalion was deployed for the transfer of Dutch land mines and installation of beach stakes. The barricades were to reach greater depths. Our men heard unpleasant things: The SS wanted to mine any trade channels, they were prolonging the war, and the like. The condition of the temporary fortifications made me think, 'I would have rather stayed behind the lines instead of looking after the fortifications.'"

At the end of the one-year formation the head of the *Wehrmachtführungsamt und Führungsstab der Wehrmacht, Generaloberst* Jodl, inspected the division in February 1944. The inspection by the *Oberbefehlshaber der Panzergruppe* "West," *General der Panzertruppen* Freiherr Geyr von Schweppenburg, followed at the Falaise military training area and a field exercise in front of the commanding *General des II. SS-Panzer-Korps, SS-Obergruppenführer*, and *General der Waffen-SS* Hausser. The 10. *SS-Panzer-Division* "Frundsberg" was cleared for deployment—and given the war situation at the time it did not take long…

Mission in Galicia

At the beginning of March 1944 the Red Army succeeded in breaching the German front of the *Heeresgruppe* "Süd" that stretched far to the west, between the 4. and 1. *Panzer-Armee* in the region of Proskuroff and Tarnopol (today Ternopil in the Ukraine), and proceeded south toward the Dniester. The situation visibly worsened when on 10 March 1944 another offensive intercepted the communication between the 1. *Panzer-Armee* and 8. *Armee* in the region of Mogilew Podolsk and Jampol.

A brief communication between the 4. and 1. *Panzer-Armee* was again intercepted by Soviet troops on 17 March 1944. One week later enemy tank forces were north of Horodenka on the Dniester! With this, the 1. *Panzer-Armee* was entrapped at the back of the Dniester[11] without a secure bridge!

Hitler's order on this day showed how unrealistic he was: the 1. *Panzer-Armee* was to hold their front to the east and northeast and reach the 4. *Panzer-Armee* at Tarnopol with an offensive, as well as fight to free the lines of communication that were heavily threatened in the meantime. The question remained, with what units? Holding the previous positions was already barely possible, and the annihilation of the 1. *Panzer-Armee* by the Red Army was only a question of a few days!

In order to obtain permission for the retreat of the 1. *Panzer-Armee* the *Oberbefehlshaber der Heeresgruppe* "Süd," *Generalfeldmarschall* Manstein,[12] flew from Lemberg (today Lviv in the Ukraine) to Berchtesgaden to Hitler on 25 March 1944. In his memoirs[13] he recalls:

> "*I added that the success of the breakthrough of the army that I planned would presuppose a counterthrust on the part of the 4.* Panzer-Armee. *For this, forces had to be supplied.*
>
> *In response, Hitler explained that he could not release any forces for this purpose. As long as he expects an invasion in the west, he cannot deploy any units there…*
>
> *When I arrived at the evening lecture, Hitler's disposition had completely changed. He began roughly with the words: 'I have considered the situation once again, I agree with your views regarding the 1.* Panzer-Armee *fighting through to the west. With a heavy heart I have decided to supply an* SS-Panzer-Korps *newly formed in the west with the 9. and 10.* SS-Panzer-Division, *as well as the 100.* Jäger-Division *and the 367.* Infanterie-Division *of the 4.* Panzer-Armee *from Hungary for the requested* Stoßgruppe…*

---

11 The Dnjstr was on average 150 to 250 m wide and had a depth of 2 – 4.5 m. The shore partly had a height of 180 m!
12 See Appendix 7
13 Manstein, Erich: Verlorene Siege, München 1979.

Early on 26 March 1944 I flew back to the Heeresgruppe…*and on the morning of 30 March 1944 I was awoken with the surprising report that Hitler's Condor machine, which* Feldmarschall *von Kleist already picked up in his headquarters, would soon be landing in Lemberg. It was to bring me together with Kleist to Obersalzberg…*

After conferment of the Swords, Hitler explained to me that he decided to assign the Heeresgruppe *to someone else (with Model[14]). In the east, the time of large-scale operations, for which I am especially suitable, has come to an end. It all comes down to rigid adherence. This new type of leadership must be introduced with a new name and a new slogan. From this, the change in leadership of the* Heeresgruppe, *whose name he also intended to change."*

Manstein's lecture with Hitler was successful! On the same day the 1. *Panzer-Armee* received the order to break through toward the east and north of the Dniester over the lower Zbrucz and Seret to the west under cover of the Front, in order to then connect to the northwest with the II. *SS-Panzer-Korps* (4. *Panzer-Armee*) advancing from the region southwest of Tarnopol.

On 2 April 1944 the OKW announced Hitler's exact instructions to fight free the 1. *Panzer-Armee*[15]:

1.) The Russian offensive in the south of the Eastern front has exceeded its high point. The Russians have worn down their units and branched apart. The time has come to bring the Russian action to an end… (sic!)

3.) The primary task of the Heeresgruppe *'Süd' is the fighting free of the 1.* Panzer-Armee *from their encirclement. The 1.* Panzer-Armee *is to continue to break through to the northwest*

From the present and newly arriving units a strong Angriffsgruppe *is to be formed in the region southeast of Lemberg, that must report at the earliest possible time with strongly concentrated forces in the southeast in order to annihilate the enemy group that broke through in the Stanislau region (today Ivano-Frankivsk in the Ukraine) and to reconnect with the 1.* Panzer-Armee. *I highly agree with* Feldmarschall *von Manstein's proposal. After joining the 1.* Panzer-Armee, *the line that was initially ordered is to be won by regional advances, to connect to the* Heeresgruppe *'Mitte' south of Kowel (today Kovel in the Ukraine) and to establish a closed Front…."*

---

14 See Appendix 7
15 OKW/GenStdH/OpAbt. (1) Tgb.Nr. 440 129/44 geh. Kdos./Chefs from 2 April 1944.

Panzer IV of the *II./SS-Panzer-Abteilung* 10 in transit.

SS-Panzer-Instandsetzungs-Abteilung 10.

Opel 3 t truck (above) – Sonder-Kfz. 9 (below).

Within the framework of the II. *SS-Panzer-Korps* (*SS-Obergruppenführer* and *General der Waffen-SS* Hausser[16]), the 10. *SS-Panzer-Division* "Frundsberg" was already alarmed on 26 March 1944 and from the Lisieux - Bernay region loaded onto the train. Through Nantes – Paris – Metz – Trier – Koblenz – Kassel – Halle – Cottbus – Breslau (today Wrocław in Poland) – Krakow the units reached Lemberg. In a motorized march through Zloczow (today Zolochiv in the Ukraine) on 3 April 1944 the sections reached the Podhojce assembly area. After the *Korpsgruppe* "Breith" (1. *Panzer-Armee*) advanced to the northwest, the II. *SS-Panzer-Korps* offensive began. Reinforced by the 367. *Infanterie-Division* and the 100. *Jäger-Division*, the 9. and 10. *SS-Panzer-Division* mustered the next day toward Buczacz (today Buchach in the Ukraine).

The distance between the *Entsatzgruppe* "Hausser" and the advancing sections of the 1. *Panzer-Armee* amounted to approximately 50 km. On 4 April 1944, in black ice and heavy snowdrifts, the 9. *SS-Panzer-Division* "Hohenstaufen," 100. *Jäger-Division*, and 10. *SS- Panzer-Division* "Frundsberg," as well as the 367. *Infanterie-Division* arrived from left to right. After intense combat the II. *SS-Panzer-Korps* could not only establish numerous bridgeheads over the Strypa until 6 April 1994, but also connect with units of the 6. *Panzer-Division* (1. *Panzer-Armee*) in Buczacz shortly after 17:00 hours with an armored group of the 10. *SS-Panzer-Division* "Frundsberg" (II. /*SSPanzer-Regiment* 10)! This success, however, was called into question by the constant counterattacks. The I./*SS-Panzer-Grenadier-Regiment* 21 advanced to Monasterzyska and the *SS-Panzer-Aufklärungs-Abteilung* 10 to Kurdwanowka. On 8 April 1944 the *SS-Panzer-Grenadier-Regiment* 22, not yet deployed, reached the streets in the region north of Buczacz, which were hardly passable because of the mud, and immediately continued to attack to the north.

10 April 1944 brought difficult missions for the entire 10. *SS-Panzer-Division*. As the division's left flank, the *SS-Panzer-Aufklärungs-Abteilung* 10 was primarily responsible for ensuring contact with the 100. *Jäger-Division*, while following toward the southeast, the *SS-Panzer-Grenadier-Regimenter* 21 and 22 advanced to the north with the support of II./*SS-Panzer-Regiment* 10. In heavy combat that involved heavy losses the daily objective could be reached. The next day the I./*SS-Panzer-Grenadier-Regiment* 21, together with the II./*SS-Panzer-Regiment* 10, arrived for the strike on Kosow (today Kosiv in the Ukraine). As of 14 April 1944 sections of the 7. *Panzer-Division* (1. *Panzer-Armee*) relieved the *SS-Panzer-Grenadier-Regiment* 21 in position, which together with sections of the *SS-Panzer-Aufklärungs-Abteilung* 10 crushed a Soviet bridgehead at Bobulince. Two days later the attack began that was led with the support of the 19. *Panzer-Division* to the south, as well as the 100. *Jäger-Division* from the north. After successfully crushing the enemy bridgeheads the front of the 1. *Panzer-Armee* at the Strypa – Pilawa line was stabilized!

---

16 See Appendix 7

For the approximately two-week mission, the losses for the 10. SS-*Panzer-Division* "Frundsberg" amounted to: 577 fallen, 1,432 wounded, and 67 missing (total: 2,076 men).

With a strength of just 18,000 men the unit had over a 10% loss—a number that reflects the severity of the combat! A former member of the *SS-Panzer-Aufklärungs-Abteilung* 10 recalls the first battles:

"In February 1944 we held an exercise in front of Generaloberst *Jodl at the Bernay airfield. Unit combat shooting followed at the Falaise training area in front of* General Geyr *and a field exercise in front of* SS-Obergruppenführer *Hausser. Combat shooting southeast of Bernay concluded training, which had lasted nearly one year. We were finally ready for deployment! It also shouldn't take much longer.*

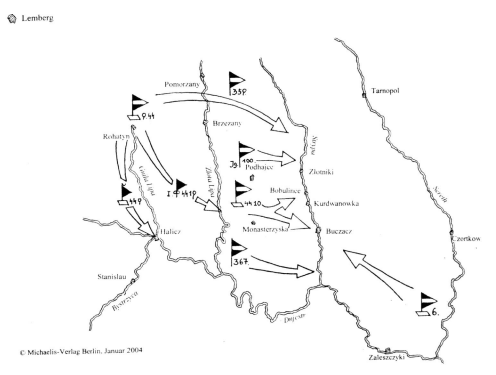

Battles of the II. *SS-Panzer-Korps* in Galicia
4-24 April 1944

At the end of March 1944 it was time. We boarded in Lisieux and left for the Eastern front for the first mission. We were to fight free the 1. Panzer-Armee *that was surrounded at Kamenez-Podolsk.*

We unloaded in Zloczow, east of Lemberg, and marched through Brezezany, in the assembly area to Podhajce. The assignment for our unit stated: Left flank protection of the division by attacking the Strypa sector north of Buczacz.

In the early afternoon hours of 5 April 1944 the section lined up. Kurdwanowka was taken during the evening hours. The 3. Kompanie *reached the Strypa and positioned combat outposts on the heights east of the Strypa. The continued line-up of the unit had come to a halt for the time being, particularly because many armored half-tracks had gotten stuck in the mud. During the afternoon the next day an enemy invasion with tanks followed in the back of the 3.* Kompanie, *which subsequently broke away from the pincer movement and set off to Kurdwanowka. Contact to the 100.* Jäger-Division, *our left neighbor, was not non-existent, likewise to our* SS-Panzer-Grenadier-Regiment 22 *that formed to the right of us. The section took up switch position on the heights east of Kurdwanowka, and on 11 April 1944 lined up for attack through Bobulincze. Driven back into defense, there was no contact to the left and right neighbors! The opponent took advantage of this and advanced on both sides of the unit far toward the west. In the night of 13 April 1944 the section escaped the pincer movement and moved again into defense positions on the heights east of Kurdwanowka. It was of little use – in the course of 14 April 1944 we were surrounded. At daybreak of 15 April 1944 an enemy invasion with tanks followed at the 3.* Kompanie. *In a counterthrust the enemy could be pushed back, and the next day we were relieved by a* Tiger-Kompanie *and together attacked again.*

Finally, there was contact with the 100. Jäger-Division, *and the* SS-Panzer-Grenadier-Regiment 21 *was pulled to the right. On 18. April 1944 the 100.* Jäger-Division *took over our positions – we became* Korpsreserve. *The first awards were conferred.*

In the night of 20 April 1944 renewed deployment of the section until 24 April 1944 – then a final withdrawal. None of us survivors will forget how we, due to lack of heavy weapons, shot with machine guns and carbines at attacking tanks or with a handful of men in a counterthrust took care of the invasion at the 3. Kompanie!

The year 1925 had withstood its baptism of fire – We were true soldiers of the Front."

Kettenkrad

Opel "Blitz" Maultier

15 cm *Panzerhaubitze* "Hummel" (above) and *Versorgungsstaffel* (below) in Galicia.

Galicia summer 1944

On 24/25 April 1944 the division was relieved by sections of the 20. *Panzer-Grenadier-Division* and 371. *Infanterie-Division*, and as *Heeresgruppenreserve* marched to the Rohatyn – Halicz region (today Halych in the Ukraine). Three days later *SS-Standartenführer* Harmel took over command of the division from *SS-Gruppenführer* and *Generalleutnant der Waffen-SS* von Treuenfeld, who a short time later became commanding *General des VI. SS-Freiwilligen-Armee-Korps* (Latvian). Harmel, who last served in the 2. *SS-Panzer-Division* "Das Reich," announced his taking up the position in an order of the day:

"*Führer and men of the 10.* SS-Panzer-Division '*Frundsberg!*'
The Reichsführer-SS *assigned me with the command of the 10.* SS-Panzer-Division '*Frundsberg.*' *Today I took over the command of the division. I am happy to be able to lead a troop in whose name the glorious tradition of the Frundsberg army lives on. Discipline and inexhaustible aggressive spirit are decisively bound with this tradition. I am proud that the young division has proven itself with dignity in the previous days of battle and has found the fullest recognition. In complete confidence in the spirit and composure of* Führer *and men I expect from the division that it integrates with dignity into the rows of the old seasoned divisions of the* Waffen-SS. *Your place shall not be the last!*
Forward for the Führer, *Nation and* Reich!*"*

On 1 May 1944, as *Heeresgruppenreserve*, the 10. *SS-Panzer-Division* received the order to transfer to the Pomorzany region (4. *Panzer-Armee*). The 9. *SS-Panzer-Division* "Hohenstaufen" was already south in the Brzezany – Podjajce region since 20 April 1944 after the advance toward Tarnopol, which was not very successful.

Already on 2 May 1944 the II. *SS-Panzer-Korps* at the command of the 4. *Panzer-Armee* ordered the battle against numerous partisan groups at the assembly areas of both *Panzer-Divisionen*:

"*In Wierzbow (11 km northwest of Brzezany) a severe gang assault occurred. A gang of approximately 200 men (members of the* Bandera-Gruppe*) is located there.*
In Swirz – Hanaczow (15 km northeast of Bobrka) there are likewise gangs with the strength of approximately 300 men, with this, according to statements from the inhabitants approximately 20 Russian parachutists. In Hanaczow positions were dug, and the parsonage fortified.
II. SS-Panzer-Korps *fought against these gangs with* Jagdkommandos *of the 9. and 10.* SS-Panzer-Division *and destroyed them.*"

The situation in the back region of the *Heeresgruppe* "Nordukraine," specifically in Galicia, differed greatly to those of the *Heeresgruppen* "Mitte" and "Nord." The Ukrainian Insurgent Army (*Ukrainska Powstanska Armiya* (UPA)), formed in 1943 historically, saw the Soviets as the prime enemy, and after the release of the Ukrainian nationalists Bandera,

Melnik, and Borrowetz from German preventative detention (since 1941), there was regular collaboration with German troops. In the hinterland of the 4. *Panzer-Armee* this nearly led to the disappearance of Soviet Partisans![17]

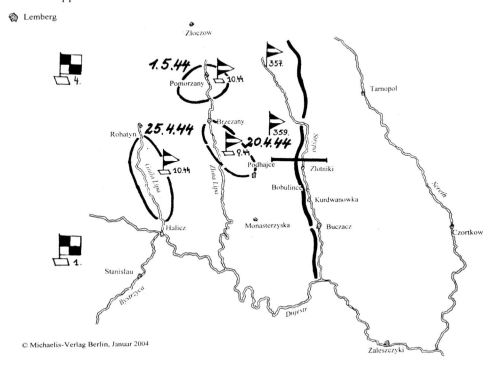

The 10. *SS-Panzer-Division* "Frundsberg" as *Heeresgruppenreserve*

On 1 June 1944 the II. *Panzer-Korps* was placed under the command of the 1. *Panzer-Armee*:

"*By order of the* Heeresgruppe *the* Generalkommando II. SS-Panzer-Korps *with the* 9. *and* 10. Panzer-Division, *as well as the* 8. Panzer-Division *tactically and officially steps under the command of the* PzAOK 1 *effective immediately. The deployment of all sections of the corps is left up to the Heeresgruppe.*"

---

17 The monthly reports of the gang situation, *Panzer-AOK* 4

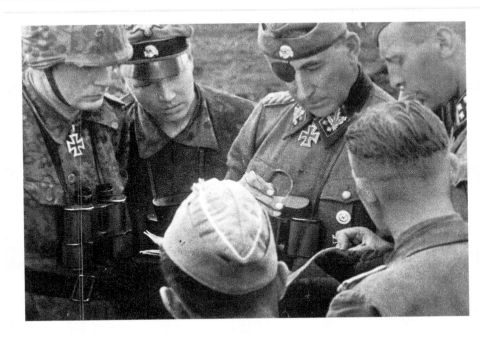

SS-Oberführer Harmel (left) and *SS-Obergruppenführer* Hausser (center).

Divisionsadjutant SS-Sturmbannführer Reinicke

Sturmgeschütze III of the *II./SS-Panzer-Regiment* 10.

On 7 June 1944 the transfer of the 10. *SS-Panzer-Division* "Frundsberg" began in the region of the 1. *Panzer-Armee*. Initially:

the *SS-Panzer-Grenadier-Regiment* 21
sections of the *SS-Panzer-Artillerie-Regiment* 10
sections of the *SS-Panzer-Pionier-Bataillon* 10
sections of the *SS-Panzer-Aufklärungs-Abteilung* 10

were detailed to the Stanislau region. However, there was no further deployment. Rather, the *SS* unit already received the order the next day to transfer to the region north of Lemberg. From there the entire II. *SS-Panzer-Korps* loaded onto the train, in order to fight against the Allied troops that had landed in Normandy since 6 June 1944.

The *Oberbefehlshaber* of the *Heeresgruppe* "Nordukraine," *Generalfeldmarschall* Model, left the II. *SS-Panzer-Korps* in an order of the day on 12 June 1944:[18]

"*Soldiers of the II.* SS-Panzer-Korps*!*
On 12 June 1944 the II. SS-Panzerkorps *with the 9.* SS-Panzer-Division '*Hohenstaufen*' *and the 10.* SS-Panzer-Division '*Frundsberg*' *is leaving the unit of the* Heeresgruppe '*Nordukraine.*'
During the time under the command of the Heeresgruppe '*Nordukraine*' *the corps in the most difficult of times have taken the principal part in the strengthening of the front and the formation of a shield for the Generalgouvernement and with this for the homeland. With the relief attack for Tarnopol and the re-establishment of contact with the 1. Panzer-Armee at Buczacz you men of the 9. and 10. SS-Panzer-Division have decisively helped to establish this shield.*
Thanks and recognition to the leadership and troop! Men of the II. SS-Panzer-Korps, *you can be proud of the successes under the command of your tried and true commanding General,* SS-Obergruppenführer *and* General der Waffen-SS *Hausser.*
The command of the Führer *calls on you for new tasks. I am certain that you will settle them with our motto in mind, no other soldier of the world is better than the soldiers of our Führer Adolf Hitler!*
My best wishes to the leadership and troop. Hail our Führer!"

Leaning towards the new guidelines of the OKH, on 2 June 1944 the *SS-FHA* announced new arrangements for *Panzer-Division* 44. In comparison to the *Panzer-Division* 43,[19] the number of tanks for each company was reduced from 22 to 17. On one hand, this meant a sparing of 40 tanks; on the other hand, naturally, a great weakening of the fighting strength of a *Panzer-Division*.

---

18 The OB of the Heeresgruppe "Nordukraine," Ia Tgb. Nr. 2781/44 geh. from 12 June 1944
19 Compare Appendix 1

Galicia 1944

SS-Oberführer Harmel in conversation with a *Hauptmann* of the *Sturzkampf-Geschwader* 77.

SS-Oberführer Harmel with Major Bruck (*Kdre. Stuka-Geschwader* 77).

The former *SS-Rottenführer* Helmut Uphoff recalls:

"I was born on 29 April 1922. I actually wanted to be a RAD-Führer. *However, the* Waffen-SS *seemed 'more successful' to me then, and in 1939 I joined the 1.* SS-Totenkopf-Rekruten-Standarte *in Dachau. I then came to the 6./6.* SS-Totenkopf-Infanterie-Regiment, *and with this unit to Norway in April 1940. On 6 July 1941 I was wounded at Salla (Karelia), and in October 1941 reported to Neuengamme for guard duty!*

As of 1943 I then belonged to the newly formed II. SS-Panzer-Korps *and was a driver of a* Kraftfahrkompanie. *In March 1944 we were on the trucks and to the Tarnopol – Lemberg region. Our 10.* SS-Panzer-Division *'Frundsberg' managed to make contact with the encircled troops of the 1.* Panzer-Armee, *and two times I got off lightly. The Russian IL 2 wanted my truck?*

At the beginning of June 1944 lighting transport to Normandy: There continuous operations on the street between the front and the ammunition and supply depot. We always drove only at night without any light – during the day the Allies bombed everything that moved!"

Ford V 8 (3 t)

Conflicts in Normandy

While the 10. *SS-Panzer-Division* "Frundsberg"—originally formed for the defense of the anticipated invasion in France, as reserves of the *Heeresgruppe* "Nordukraine" were located in the Pomorzany region—respectively marched in sections into the Stanislau region, and on 6 June 1944 the Allied invasion in Normandy began.

The Invasion
6 June 1944

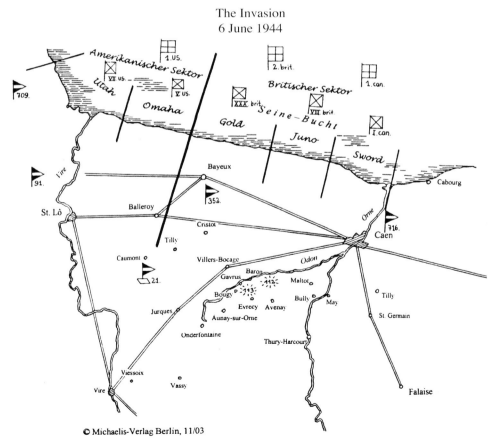

© Michaelis-Verlag Berlin, 11/03

The landing took place after heavy air and ship bombing in the region between the mouth of the Seine and Cherbourg. The Allied operation was launched at 1:00 hours at night with paratroopers. The actual invasion followed between 3:00 and 3:30 hours at Ebbe, so that the German littoral obstacles did not interfere, in five sectors of the beach: Utha, Omaha, Gold, Juno, and Sword. British and Canadian units came to shore on both sides of the Orne, and the Americans to the mouth of the Vire and on the Cotentin peninsula north of St. Lo.

In the region of the AOK 7 on the evening of 6 June 1944 the situation east of the Orne was resolved by the 711. *Infanterie-Division*, reinforced with sections of the 21. *Panzer-Division*; however, west of the river was a 10 km deep British bridgehead. For this on 7 June 1944 the AOK 7 ordered the counterthrust of the I. *SS-Panzer-Korps* with the 21. *Panzer-Division*, 12. *SS-Panzer-Division* "Hitlerjugend," and the *Panzer-Lehr-Division*, in order to throw the enemy located west of the Orne into the ocean again, according to Rommel's plans. The Allied absolute air supremacy hindered the German offensive. The KTB of the AOK 1 noted on 8 June 1944:

"Because there still is no contact with the I. SS-Panzerkorps *that after yesterday's postponed attack in the morning hours of 8 June was to muster from the assembly area north of Caen toward the cost, the* Oberbefehlshaber *gave a personal briefing on the situation at the Calvados bridgehead at the I.* SS-Panzerkorps *command post. There was still no report in the afternoon hours on the situation in the Caen combat area. It seemed as though the attack of the I.* SS-Panzerkorps *still had not begun."*

When British units did not succeed in advancing into the northern parts of Caen and capturing Bayeux to the west, the *Panzer-Lehr-Division* received the order to muster at Bayeux. The members of the 12. *SS-Panzer-Division* "Hitlerjugend," mostly just 18 years old, prevented a continued advance of the opponent in the most difficult battles at Caen and Christot. Because there was no advancement here, the British 2nd Army transferred their focus of attack to the west, in the Tilly region.

During heavy combat on the front, the Allies constantly landed new troops in France: a total of 300,000 men in the first six days; one week after the landing the beachhead was already 100 km wide and 30 km deep!

On 11 June 1944, in the course of the critical situational development in Normandy, Hitler ordered, among others, the II. *SS-Panzer-Korps*, which was to participate in a planed operation of attack in the Kowel region, to immediately move back to the west. The 10. *SS-Panzer-Division* "Frundsberg," assembled in the region north of Lemberg, unloaded the next day at the Sokol and Krystynopol (today Chervonohrad in the Ukraine) train stations, and as of 20 June 1944 reached the Nancy – Bar le Duc region (southwest of Metz) through Jaroslau – Oppeln (today Opole in Poland) – Breslau – Cottbus – Cologne – Straßbourg.

On the same day Hitler ordered the *Oberbefehlshaber* "West" to split the front between the British 2ⁿᵈ Army and American 1ˢᵗ Army in the Caumont – Bayeux region, with the I. and II. *SS-* as well as the XXXXVIII. *Panzer-Korps*, and destroy the American east wing at Balleroy in order to then close in and annihilate the British units. With the material superiority of heavy weapons and aircraft of the Allies an illusionary order—the "*Gesetz des Handelns*"—was conclusively on the side of the Anglo-American units.

While the U.S. troops attempted to seize Cherbourg, British units formed once again to seize the strategically crucial Caen. They advanced east of the Orne (northeast of Caen) in the region of the 16. *Luftwaffen-Feld-Division* and the 21. *Panzer-Division*, and at Tilly-sur-Suelles (west of Caen) over the Odenbach. The objective was to close in over the heights to the Orne and surround Caen. As a result of this the planned German major offensive in the Caumont – Bayeux region had to be abandoned. In fact, the divisions were deployed for attack in the east. Here the positions of the 12. *SS-Panzer-Division* "Hitlerjugend" were partly lost due to the constant British tank attacks, supported by bombing and heavy artillery fire, and additionally, fighting broke out for the strategically critical Hill 112.

On 29 June 1944 the quickly deteriorating situation led to a hasty deployment of the II. *SS-Panzer-Korps* (*SS-Gruppenführer* and *Generalleutnant der Waffen-SS* Bittrich[20]) to the west flank of the British troops advancing southeast. The 9. *SS-Panzer-Division* "Hohenstaufen" attacked left of the street Villers – Bocage, and from the right the 10. *SS-Panzer-Division* "Frundsberg," reinforced by the *SS-Panzer-Grenadier-Regiment* 4 "Der Führer." The latter had at its command:

	Führer	*Unterführer*	Men	Total[21]
Actual Strength:	374	2,266	10,912	12,552
Required Strength:	614	3,923	13,260	17,791

At 14:30 hours, from the Neuilly region the *SS-Panzer-Grenadier-Regiment* 22 formed, at St. Honorine the *SS-Panzer-Grenadier-Regiment* 21, and from Maizet the *SS-Panzer-Aufklärungs-Abteilung* 10 in collaboration with the 12. *SS-Panzer-Division* "Hitlerjugend" toward Hill 112. Reinforced by sections of the *SS-Panzer-Regiment* 10 and the *SS-Panzer-Pionier-Bataillon*, the *SS-Panzer-Grenadier-Regiment* 22 succeeded in occupying Gavrus

---

20 The previous commanding *General des II. SS-Panzer-Korps*, *SS-Obergruppenführer* and *General der Waffen-SS* Hausser had taken over the command of the 7. *Armee*.
21 With this, the unit had over roughly 75% of the required strength at their disposal – with the *Führer* approximately 40% was lacking.

after erratic and difficult battles. The *SS-Panzer-Grenadier-Regiment* 21, also supported by sections of the *SS-Panzer-Regiment* 10 and the *SS-Panzer-Pionier-Bataillon* 10, pushed forward against Hill 113 and was able to seize Vieux through Avenay. Finally, on 30 June 1944 the regiment, together with the 12. *SS-Panzer-Division* "Hitlerjugend" attacking from the east, was able to occupy the strategically significant Hill 112.

The Deployment of the 10. *SS-Panzer-Division*
29 June – 1 August 1944

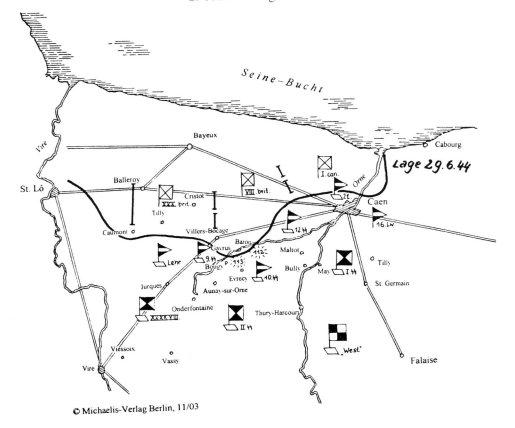

© Michaelis-Verlag Berlin, 11/03

On 2 July 1944, as the *SS-Panzer-Pionier-Bataillon* 9 took over the positions of the II./ *SS-Panzer-Grenadier-Regiment* 22 at Gavrus, the II. *Bataillon* was initially pulled from the front; it was, however, deployed the next day at Fontaine. Here the British troops attempted to invade the area between the 10. and 12. *SS-Panzer-Division*, and were able to occupy Maltot. However, in heavy combat, sections of both *SS-Panzer-Divisionen* succeeded in recapturing the town. At the same time, there was another counterattack of the English on Hill 112. The constant artillery fire surpassed the battles at Verdun during World War I! All available weapons of the *SS-Panzer-Artillerie-Regiment* 10 and the *SS-Panzer-Flak-Abteilung10*, as well as the II./*SS-Panzer-Regiment* 10, together with *Grenadiere* of the *SS-Panzer-Grenadier-Regiment* 21 made it possible to hold the hill. A former member of the II./*SS-Panzer-Regiment* 10 recalls:

"*On 30 October 1943 I was called up as a war volunteer to the* SS-Sturmgeschütz-Ausbildungs- und Ersatz-Abteilung *on the Heidelager military training area at Debica. At this time the commander of this unit was* SS-Sturmbannführer *Sinn. After recruitment and gun training I was transferred to the* SS-Sturmgeschütz-Abteilung *10 at the beginning of April 1944. After arriving at 'Frundsberg' we learned that this unit didn't exist! So we were assigned to the II.* Abteilung *of the* Panzer-Regiment, *whose 7. and 8.* Kompanie *were equipped with* Sturmgeschütze. *Because we showed up with a lot of 'Debicians' there, it was not possible to accommodate everyone in both companies. To my pleasure I ended up with the 6.* Kompanie *(Chief:* SS-Untersturmführer *Quandel).* SS-Untersturmführer *Klinkmann and* SS-Unterscharführer *Knape did retraining with us. At this time the 6.* Kompanie *was situated in Rohatyn. Shortly after our arrival we transferred to Bryczcow.*

We were no longer deployed – rather, we immediately transferred to France. The rail transport continued to Paris and from there in a motorized march. While the company carried out their first attack at Maltot – Maison Blanche, I initially remained at the baggage train in Montigny, in order to soon be deployed at Hill 113 at Evrecy as a Panzerwarner. *For this I received the EK 2. Already 48 hours later I found myself in the* SS-Korps-Lazarett *502 at Domfront with a shell splinter injury on my face. Because I do not tolerate the smell of Lysol and frankincense very well – the military hospital was accommodated in a cloister– I was soon with the company again, who at this time was deployed to Hill 112. I came to the crew of* SS-Unterscharführer *Knappe. In the meantime we had a new* Kompanieführer, *to whom the 6.* Kompanie *owed some senseless and avoidable losses of dead and wounded due to especially snappy orders. It soon got him. His death was just as senseless, and we were happy to receive Quandel again. After the mission on Hill 112 I was with various crews of the 6., but came again to* SS-Unterscharführer *Knappe. Battles at Auney-sur-Oden, La Lande-sur-Odon, Onte Fontaine, Domfront, Longley, Flers, and Vassey followed, partially assigned within the company, partially to other units.*"

On 8 July 1944 the 9. *SS-Panzer-Division* "Hohenstaufen" was detached from the 277. *Infanterie-Division*, in order to be on hand as a mobile reserve in the Caen combat area. Sections of the *Grenadier-Regiment* 991 also took over positions of the III./*SS-Panzer-Grenadier-Regiment* 21 at Gavrus. When on the next day the 12. *SS-Panzer-Division* "Hitlerjugend" cleared Caen of British troops after a heavy bomb attack in Normandy, a critical situation arose again in the area of the 10. *SS-Panzer-Division* "Frundsberg." The heavy *SS-Panzer-Abteilung* 102 (Tiger) was able to settle the situation once more. On 10 July 1944 the opponent attacked Hill 112 with a large use of materiel—here the II./*SS-Panzer-Abteilung* 10 initially prevented a fiasco! Two days later the British tanks were able to reach Hill 112. Sections of the heavy *SS-Panzer-Abteilung* 102 that were immediately deployed stabilized the situation again. At the same time, the *SS-Panzer-Grenadier-Regiment* 19 received the order to reinforce the III./*SS-Panzer-Grenadier-Regiment* 22 on Hill 112. When on 18 July 1944 the battalion was pulled from the main front, their strength amounted to fewer than 50 men! With this, in the previous three weeks there was an approximate 90% loss (sic!). Other units at the main front did not look much different!

Both first battalions of the *SS-Panzer-Grenadier-Regiment* 22 had already relieved the *SS-Panzer-Grenadier-Regiment* 20 of the 9. *SS-Panzer-Division* "Hohenstaufen" in Maltot on 15 July 1944. The *SS-Panzer-Grenadier-Regiment* 21 (without the I. *Bataillon*, which was located at Honorine in reserve) was again on 16 July 1944 in heavy defensive battles with enemy troops advancing from the Gavrus region, and could only maintain the positions east of Hill 113 with the support of the II./*SS-Panzer-Regiment* 10. On this day the *Wehrmachtbericht* reported:

"In the battles for Caen the 9. SS-Panzer-Division 'Hohenstaufen' under the command of SS-Standartenführer Stadler and the 10. SS-Panzer-Division 'Frundsberg' under the command of SS-Oberführer Harmel together with the troops of the army have distinguished themselves with exceptional bravery. In defense and attack both divisions have inflicted great losses of man and materiel on the enemy. In doing so, through these divisions altogether 140 tanks were put out of action."

After the opponent was able to invade Gavrus by the 277. *Infanterie-Division* fighting left of the 10. *SS-Panzer-Division* "Frundsberg," sections of the 9. *SS-Panzer-Division* "Hohenstaufen" that had only just pulled out were detached back to the main front. When the British troops mustered east of the Orne for a major offensive on 18 July 1944, the main front ran in front of the 10. *SS-Panzer-Division* with the left border (277. *Infanterie-Division* with sections of the 9. *SS-Panzer-Division*) from Hill 113 to west of Maltot.

The right neighbor was now the 272. *Infanterie-Division*, which relieved the battered 12. *SS-Panzer-Division* "Hitlerjugend." Because the opponent was able to break through the front of the 272. *Infanterie-Division* on 21 July 1944 and advanced before May, the *SS-Panzer-Aufklärungs-Abteilung* 10, among others, was detached to the region.

While east of the Orne the most intense battles were taking place, west of the river there were practically only localized operations of both sides. The plan of the Commander in Chief of the Allied forces in Europe, General Eisenhower, to wear out the feared German tank divisions at Caen in trench warfare was partially fulfilled. They were unable to pull out in order to prevent the breakthrough of the American units to central France.

When the front around Caen was somewhat stabilized, at the end of July 1944 the immediate relief of the II. *SS-Panzer-Korps* (9. and 10. *SS-* as well as the 21. *Panzer-Division*) began in order to transfer as a mobile combat unit to the Aunay-sur-Orne region (approximately 30 km southwest of Caen). The 10. *SS-Panzer-Division* "Frundsberg" was relieved by the 271. *Infanterie-Division*.

Already two days later the British troops succeeded in breaking through the German front in the area between the right flank of the 7. *Armee* (II. *Fallschirm-Korps*) and the left flank of the 5. *Panzer-Armee* (LXXIV. *Armee-Korps*) and advanced toward Vire. As a result, the 10. *SS-Panzer-Division* "Frundsberg" received the order on 1 August 1944 to settle the enemy invasion at Coulvain in a counterthrust, and then together with the 9. *SS-* and 21. *Panzer-Division* close the gaps in the front that had come about between the 7. and 5. *Panzer-Armee*.

While the majority of the 10. *SS-Panzer-Division* were marching, an advance party consisting of:

-        II./*SS-Panzer-Regiment* 10
-        *SS-Panzer-Aufklärungs-Abteilung* 10
-        3./*SS-Panzer-Pionier-Bataillon* 10

arrived at the new main front under the command of *SS-Sturmbannführer* Paetsch and occupied positions between Mesnil-Auzouf and Jurques on the night of 1 August 1944. The left neighbor was sections of the 21. *Panzer-Division*, the right neighbor the 326. *Infanterie-Division*, likewise reinforced by sections of the 21. *Panzer-Division*. After the majority of the 10. *SS-Panzer-Division* "Frundsberg" had reached the Ondefontaine assembly area during the night of 2 August 1944, the next morning the advance on the British flank began. The battles for the Hills 321, 301, and 248 were difficult, and were bitterly fought by both sides.

To the southwest the opponent was able to pierce through the German main front and advance into the Burcy – Chenedolle region. Though the German command was successful in closing the main front again, thus encircling three enemy divisions, the material superiority and strength of the Allied troops prevented a resounding success. Because the emaciated German troops were no longer able to implement the ordered straightening of the front line north of Vire – Burcy – Presles – Estry with their available forces, on the night of 4 August 1944 the 10. *SS-Panzer-Division* "Frundsberg" received a transfer order from the main front and were to march from Jurques to the region approximately 20 km south.

The Deployment of the 10. *SS-Panzer-Division*
1-5 August 1944

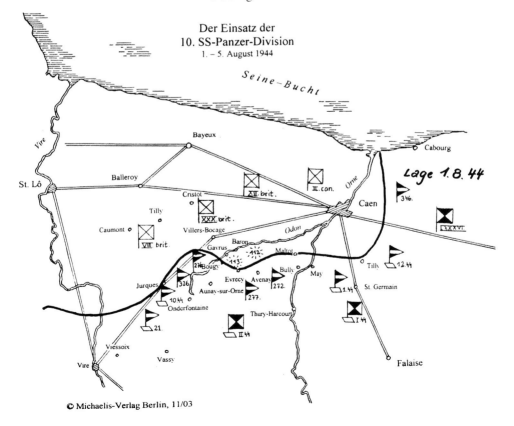

© Michaelis-Verlag Berlin, 11/03

Sonder-Kfz. 7 (8 t.)

Ernst Weinlich served as of 30 May 1943 in the *SS-Artillerie-Regiment* 10 as driving instructor and motorist. On 3 August 1944 he was wounded at Ondefontaine.

The service record book of *SS-Unterscharführer* Weinlich.

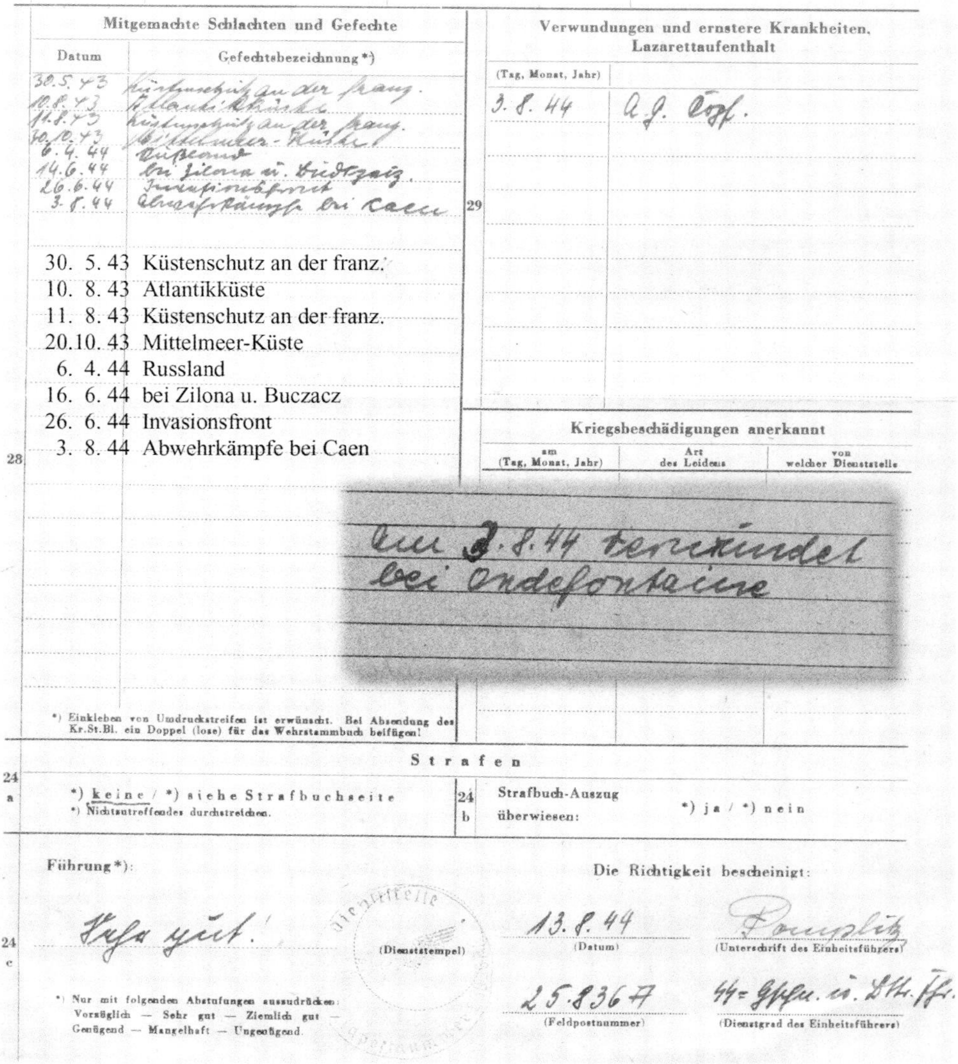

Mitgemachte Schlachten und Gefechte		Verwundungen und ernstere Krankheiten, Lazarettaufenthalt		
Datum	Gefechtsbezeichnung *)	(Tag, Monat, Jahr)		

(handwritten entries:)

```
30.5.43  Küstenschutz an der franz.
10.8.43  Atlantikküste
11.8.43  Küstenschutz an der franz.
20.10.43 Mittelmeer-Küste
6.4.44   Russland
16.6.44  bei Zilona u. Buczacz
26.6.44  Invasionsfront
3.8.44   Abwehrkämpfe bei Caen
```

3. 8. 44   Q.J. Cof.

28		30. 5. 43 Küstenschutz an der franz.
		10. 8. 43 Atlantikküste
		11. 8. 43 Küstenschutz an der franz.
		20.10. 43 Mittelmeer-Küste
		6. 4. 44 Russland
		16. 6. 44 bei Zilona u. Buczacz
		26. 6. 44 Invasionsfront
		3. 8. 44 Abwehrkämpfe bei Caen

Kriegsbeschädigungen anerkannt

am (Tag, Monat, Jahr)	Art des Leidens	von welcher Dienststelle

(handwritten:) am 3.8.44 verwundet bei Ondefontaine

*) Einkleben von Umdruckstreifen ist erwünscht. Bei Absendung des Kr.St.Bl. ein Doppel (lose) für das Wehrstammbuch beifügen!

S t r a f e n

| 24 a | *) k e i n e / *) s i e h e S t r a f b u c h s e i t e *) Nichtzutreffendes durchstreichen. | 24 b | Strafbuch-Auszug überwiesen: *) j a / *) n e i n |

Führung*):   Die Richtigkeit bescheinigt:

| 24 c | *Sehr gut!*   (Dienststempel) | 13.8.44 (Datum) | (Unterschrift des Einheitsführers) |
| | *) Nur mit folgenden Abstufungen ausdrücken: Vorzüglich — Sehr gut — Ziemlich gut — Genügend — Mangelhaft — Ungenügend. | 25.836 (Feldpostnummer) | ᛋᛋ=Hstf. u. Sta.Kp. (Dienstgrad des Einheitsführers) |

Stammblatt and *Stammkarte* excerpt of *SS-Unterscharführer* Weinlich.

Already the next morning the 10. *SS-Panzer-Division* arrived at Chenedolle with multiple *Kampfgruppen*. After initial minor successes, however, the counterattack soon remained under heavy enemy artillery and ground attack pilot fire. A continuation of the attack was futile with the capture of Vire by British troops on 7 August 1944, and the front on the line south of Vire – Chenedolle taken back. The 10. *SS-Panzer-Division* "Frundsberg" immediately received a new order to transfer to the St. Clement – Ger region to be at the command of the 7. *Armee*.

In the meantime, the 3ʳᵈ U.S. Army had broken through the German positions at Avranches, and could thereby advance in the free region of France. Hitler ordered the immediate counterattack of the 7. *Armee* (*SS-Oberstgruppenführer* and *Generaloberst der Waffen-SS* Hausser), with which the front was to be closed again to the coast, and the enemy forces that broke through were to be annihilated. In the face of the Allied superiority an incredibly unreasonable demand!

Deployment of the 10. *SS-Panzer-Division* at Vire

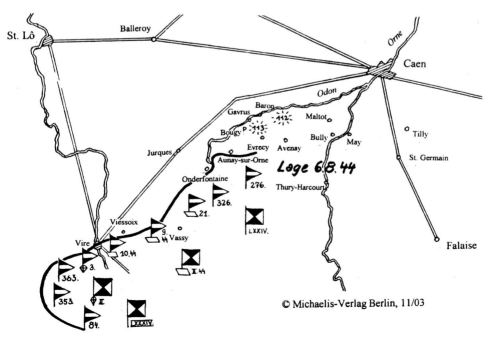

© Michaelis-Verlag Berlin, 11/03

Under the code name "Lüttich," the XXXXVII. *Panzer-Korps* (*General der Panzertruppen* Freiherr von Funck[22]) with the 2. and 116. *Panzer-Division*, as well as the 2. *SS-Panzer-Division* and the remainder of the 17. *SS-Panzer-Grenadier-Division*, had to advance from the Sourdeval – St. Clément – Barenton region on the night of 6 August 1944 and reach Avranches in two days. The II. *SS-Panzer-Korps* was intended as a second wave that was to follow with the 9. and 10., as well as sections of the 1. *SS-Panzer-Division*. To the right of the XXXXVII. *Panzer-Korps* stood the LXXXIV. *Armee-Korps* with the 363., 353., 343., and 84. *Infanterie-Division*, and to the left the LVIII. *Panzer-Korps* with the 275. *Infanterie- und Panzer-Lehr-Division*.

After the 2. *SS-Panzer-Division* "Das Reich" was able to occupy Mortain and other *Angriffsgruppen* advanced roughly 20 km west in bad weather, the weather improved and allowed for the deployment of the Allied air force. As a result, already up until 8 August 1944 approximately 100 German *Kampfwagen* were put out of action (sic!). Therefore, the *Oberbefehlshaber* "West," *Generalfeldmarschall* Kluge, ordered the cessation of further attacks and the retreat to the developed starting positions; Operation "Lüttich" had resulted in nothing but a further weakening of the already battered German combat units! Taking advantage of this weakening, the American 3ʳᵈ Army arrived the next day for the offensive.

The 10. *SS-Panzer-Division* "Frundsberg" was placed under the command of the LVIII. *Panzer-Korps* and received the order to recapture Barenton and block the street Mortain – Domfront. Furthermore, contact to the 2. *SS-Panzer-Division* "Das Reich" at Mortain was to be established and its southern flank covered. The counterthrust of the *SS-Panzer-Grenadier-Regiment* 22 together with the *SS-Panzer-Pionier-Bataillon* 10, as well as the II./*SS-Panzer-Regiment* 10 on Barenton on 9 August 1944 remained north of the town in heavy combat with strong American troops. Also, to the east the *SS-Panzer-Grenadier-Regiment* 21 was likewise involved in heavy resistance combat with U.S.troops advancing north—the Allied plan to widely encircle the German troops was already apparent.

On 11 August 1944 the American troops succeeded again in capturing Montain, and the next day the 10. *SS-Panzer-Division* "Frundsberg" had to pull back toward the southeast to the line Placite – le Buissonnière – Lonlay. In the evening the division reported the following combat strength:

SS-Panzer-Grenadier-Regiment 21	approximately 500 men
SS-Panzer-Grenadier-Regiment 22	approximately 250 men
SS-Panzer-Pionier-Bataillon 10	approximately 150 men
SS-Panzer-Aufklärungs-Abteilung 10	approximately 350 men

22 See Appendix 7

Above: *SS-Panzer-Grenadiere* on a *Pkw* Horch. Below: 2 cm Flak on a *Sonder-Kfz.* 10 of the *SS-Panzer-Flak-Abteilung* 10.

In the Falaise pocket.

SS-Panzer-Regiment 10	8 tanks
SS-Panzer-Flak-Abteilung 10	9 Flak 8.8 cm
SS-Panzer-Artillerie-Regiment 10	25 barrels
	(8 Sfl. "Hummel")

At a total strength then of approximately 6,500 men, the *SS* unit had an approximate 50% loss in the roughly six weeks since 29 June 1944 (the actual strength then: approximately 13,500 men). The personnel and materiel losses in the combatant troop amounted to almost 80% (sic!).

Deployment of the 10. *SS-Panzer-Division* at Domfront

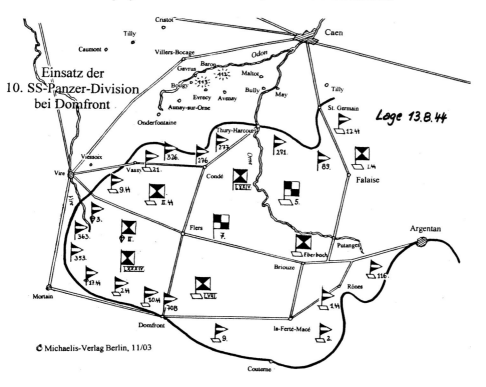

When on 14 August 1944 U.S. troops were able to capture Domfront and occupy the dominating hills north of the city, SS-*Oberführer* Harmel ordered a limited counterthrust with the last eight tanks of the *SS-Panzer-Regiment* 10. With this, at least a further retreat of the division could be secured at short notice. Things started happening very quickly: after the 10. *SS-Panzer-Division* was to be supplied to the 5. *Panzer-Armee* in the region north of Argentan, the order to ensure the flow of the 7. *Armee* in a mobile *Kampfgruppe* could not be carried out because the opponent reached the region earlier!

On the night of 16 August 1944 the 10. *SS-Panzer-Division* "Frundsberg" transferred to the Putanges region (approximately 18 km west of Argentan) and was placed under the command of the LXXXIV. *Armee-Korps* (*General der Infanterie* Elfeldt). In the following night the remainder of the division was to head north over the Orne and march to the region of Villedieu les Bailleul (approximately 3km southwest of Trun).

Things started to happen quickly—on 17 August 1944 Canadian units captured Falaise, and when two days later the Polish 1ˢᵗ Tank Division established contact with the XV U.S. Corps at Chambois, the remnants of four German *Armee-Korps* with approximately 80,000 men were encircled in the Falaise pocket.

Deployment of the 10. *SS-Panzer-Division* "Frundsberg" within the framework of the LXXXIV. *Armee-Korps* in the Falaise pocket

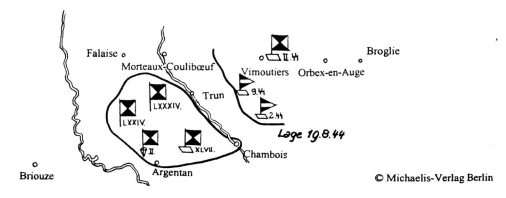

Already during the next night of 19 August 1944 the encircled *Armee-Korps* between Chambois and St. Lambert (approximately 3km northwest of Chambois) arrived over the Dives for the breakthrough to the east. From there the II. *SS-Panzer-Korps encountered them.* The situation during the escape was catastrophic for the encircled soldiers. With the saying run for your lives, there no longer existed any discipline or order! Streets were used by multiple convoys simultaneously and continuously jammed. Under heavy, constant Allied artillery and ground attack pilot fire individuals attempted to turn around and proceed elsewhere. It came to apocalyptic scenes.

Because an organized command of the units was no longer possible, *Kampfgruppen* were formed from motorized units of various divisions that were to force the breakthrough through the enemy main front. From the remainder of the *SS-Panzer-Aufklärungs-Abteilung* 10, as well as the I./*SS-Panzer-Grenadier-Regiment* 21, the *SS-Kampfgruppe* "Brinkmann" was formed, which under the leadership of the *Kommandeur der SS-Panzer-Aufklärungs-Abteilung* 10 *SS-Sturmbannführer* Brinkmann was placed under the command of the II. *Fallschirmjäger-Korps.* The severely injured *Oberbefehlshaber* of the 7. *Armee*, *SS-Oberstgruppenführer* und *Generaloberst der Waffen-SS* Hausser, was also located here.

First sections of the 10. *SS-Panzer-Division* "Frundsberg" that set over the Dives were placed under the command of the 2. *Panzer-Division* (*General der Panzertruppen von* Lüttwitz) within the framework of the I. *SS-Panzer-Korps.* Next to this *SS-Kampfgruppe* "Brinkmann" was the *Kampfgruppe/SS-Panzer-Grenadier-Regiment* 21 (remainder of the II. and III./*SS-Panzer-Grenadier-Regiment* 21, as well as the *SS-Panzer-Pionier-Bataillon* 10) and the *Kampfgruppe/SS-Panzer-Grenadier-Regiment* 22 (remainder of the three battalions of the regiment and division troops).

In the morning hours of 21 August 1944 the escape occurred—approximately 50,000 German soldiers were taken captive, 20,000 succeeded in breaking through, and 10,000 remained behind as fallen soldiers on the battlefield. The 5. *Panzer-Armee* recorded the following strengths on this day in the war diary:[23]

> "*1.* SS-Panzer-Korps *with*
>> *10.* SS-Panzer-Division: *weak* Fußteile, *strength not yet known, no tanks, no artillery*
>> *12.* SS-Panzer-Division: *300 men, 10 tanks, no artillery*
>> *1.* SS-Panzer-Division: *temporarily nothing available*
>> *2.* Panzer-Division: *infantry strength unknown, no tanks, no artillery*

---

23 KTB der 5. *Panzer-Armee* from 16-31 August 1944.

II. SS-Panzer-Korps *with*

> *1* Regiment *(probably without heavy weapons) and ten tanks.*
> *2.* SS-Panzer-Division: *450 men, 15 tanks, 6 barrels*
> *9.* SS-Panzer-Division: *460 men, 20-25 tanks, 20 barrels*
> *116.* Panzer-Division: *1 battalion, 12 tanks, no artillery"*

A day earlier Hitler authorized the 5. *Panzer-Armee* and the 1. *Armee* to pull back to the Seine in order to form a new front. For the 10. *SS-Panzer Division* this meant the retreat toward Rouen. A former *Führer* of the *SS-Panzer-Pionier-Bataillon* 10 recalls:

"*On 17 August 1944, after my* Beiwagenkrad *was hopelessly wedged in convoys during the night hours, we fumbled forward in order to search to make contact with sections of the LAH. But the opponent took away all of our worries – the opponent was already marching toward us on a parallel street with tank convoys and infantry. In a careful retreat, we were shot at by a patrol from a short distance. I was wounded and picked up by a Sanka (SPW). The Red Cross flag that a wounded soldier held was respected by the fighter-bombers. In the evening, the first treatment at a dressing station of the* Luftwaffe. *At dawn I was awakened by a young* Unterarzt *with the words: 'If you do not want to be taken captive, you must go, we have the order to hand over the wounded with medical personnel to the opponent.'*

Soon I had to struggle my way into a slit trench of a small unit; later I ended up at a Wespen-Batterie *of the LAH, from where I was brought to the command post of the LAH. Around evening the returning masses of vehicles began. Only with a drawn pistol the Ib accommodated me in an automobile of the* Feldgendarmerie, *later I was in a general's Horch that was following a heavy repair squad car. The older driver explained to me that his general was already in front. What I experienced this night can hardly be described!*

Insanity, hysteria, and force had gripped the convoys, the larger ones ate the smaller ones, and all the more the victim with continuous air attacks and heavy artillery fire of all caliber. At dawn our car came across a small convoy that helplessly stopped on the street. In front of us a large hill. Left of the street an orchard in which paratroopers retreat. Firing from tanks rumble. Brief assessment at the 'General's car.' On my mark, with 80 m distance and the utmost speed over the hill. We made it through, were able to cover a large distance and disappeared into wooded areas. Later the journey was continued in an ambulance bus. In good spirits the Stabsarzt *gave me a cigarette. In front of Bernay in a curvy stretch with mines a combat engineer vehicle was burning. The bus remained on the street, the wounded got off and laid on a small slope, everyone was wearing bandages but hardly a complete uniform. We were hardly mindful of fighter-bombers…*

Then – howling motors, our bus was already on fire and within a minute the small group of wounded were fired at with Bordkanonen and everything that still moved was preyed upon.

Somehow I reached Rouen and was moved once more when a French woman shyly looked around and then handed the wounded a bag with cookies in the Sanka."

At Elbeuf, as of 24 August 1944 the first gradually arriving *Trosseinheiten* and somewhat later *Kampfeinheiten* set over the Seine, and until the end of the month assembled in the Beauvais region. Here the division officially went under the command of the LXXXI. *Armee-Korps*.

For the retreat *SS-Oberführer* Harmel formed two *Kampfgruppen* from the remaining men of his division in the Montdidier-Fescamps region:

- *SS-Kampfgruppe* "Schultz"
  Remainder of both *SS-Panzer-Grenadier-Regiment* 21 and 22
  Sections of the *SS-Panzer-Aufklärungs-Abteilung* 10
  Sections of the *SS-Panzer-Artillerie-Regiment* 10
- *SS-Kampfgruppe* "Paetsch"
  Remainder of the *SS-Panzer-Regiment* 10
  Sections of the *SS-Panzer-Aufklärungs-Abteilung* 10
  Sections of the *SS-Pionier-Bataillon* 10
  SS-Flak-Abteilung 10

Because the 10. *SS-Panzer-Division* "Frundsberg" did not make contact with the LXXXI. *Armee-Korps* despite the ordered placement at its command, on 30 August 1944 they came under the command of the coincidentally arriving I. *SS-Panzer-Korps*. The commanding general, SS-*Obergruppenführer* and *General der Waffen-SS* Kepper,[24] ordered *SS-Oberführer* Harmel to initially take position on the Somme between Corbie and Peronne. On 31 August 1944 the *SS-Kampfgruppe* "Schultze" subsequently initially took up position at a main front at Corbie, however, they already had to pull back toward Albert until the evening. In heavy street and house combat, *SS-Obersturmbannführer* Schultze, among others, fell—the remainder of the *Kampfgruppe* struggled through to the east on the night of 1 September 1944. The *SS-Kampfgruppe* "Paetsch" was initially situated at Peronne and retreated to Bepaume until 1 September 1944, and the following night to Cambrai.

The remainder of the 10. *SS-Panzer-Division* "Frundsberg" reached the Wavre region through Mons on 3/4 September 1944 and was placed under the command of the II. *SS-Panzer-Korps*. *SS-Oberführer* (as of 7 September 1944: *SS-Brigadeführer* and *Generalmajor der Waffen-SS*) Harmel initially received the order to move into a bridgehead position at Maastricht, and then, as of 6 September 1944 transfer with the remainder of the division to the Arnhem region for replenishment.

---

24 See Appendix 7

A former member of the I./*SS-Panzer-Grenadier-Regiment* 21 recalls:

"*Since 5 May 1943 I served as* Schirrmeister *with the I./21 and trained drivers and* Instandsetzungtrupps. *As of 15 August 1944 there was no longer any organization! On this day,* SS-Unterscharführer *Huber was gunned down by fighter-bombers on his motorcycle as he was bringing us fuel for the attack on Mortain.*

Our battalion came only to Domfront – here with the staff I also lost my I-Trupp. SS-Unterscharführer *Hirsch lost his right foot from a direct hit. The battalion had great losses. Our doctor, Dr. Peters, from Unna was taken into American captivity with 35 severely injured. Sankas no longer came through – they were either fired at by fighter-bombers or French snipers!*

At 20:00 hours on 15 August 1944 SS-Obersturmführer *Barth came to us and announced our destination. We were to battle our way to St. Albert and assemble there. Because we were only able to march at night, we couldn't waste any time and had to obtain fuel as much as possible.*

We weren't even five km away until we were in a flank combat from the south with the Americans. We had 35 Schützenpanzerwagen *and approximately 30 trucks, and we picked up paratroopers, navy, and infantrymen and waged war on our own. The next morning we made it to Trun. But the path here was blocked due to carpet bombing on the city, and the enemy was already pressing from Argentan.*

At Falaise we gathered fuel from the air force in the morning and already exchanged fire with the Tommies for the cigarettes! It was still dark, my guard had fallen asleep, and I was finished with refueling. Then someone said to me 'Landser, *give me a light,' and when my lighter flashed, I was looking into the face of a Tommy. He immediately yelled 'Hands up!' – I was also of the same opinion, but out of fear I released a smoke grenade from my trouser pocket and the magic began: 75 liters of 'flame oil' and our MG 42 and we were through!*

At Vimoutiers we encountered SS-Oberstgruppenführer *Hausser and* SS-Oberführer *Harmel. Each* Landser *there had to have a rifle and munitions on his person because signs of disintegration of the German army were becoming apparent. Two tanks and my Flammenwerfer-* and *Kampfwagenkanone-Wagen brought the resistance of the Englishmen with great luck and we got through to Orbec in one piece. Here* SS-Oberführer *Harmel told us that the enemy was already occupying Evreux. Orbec – Bernay was the valley of death.*

But we also learned something. When the fighter-bombers attacked the old flour cart of bakery and needed 21 approaches, to find peace, we used a 2 kg smoke grenade; this was also a sign for the fighter-bombers that they had achieved their goal.

At Bernay a military hospital with 200-300 wounded was gunned down by the Americans.

On the evening of 23 August 1944 through Bernay we had found the marked path that left Brionne to the west. I can no longer remember the exact name of the town because we arrived late at night. I heard that around 22:00 hours Schützenpanzer and automobiles were taking off to pick up the rest of the Kampfgruppe. I had the task of allocating fuel and oil and monitoring the refueling of the motor vehicles.

In the morning provisions were handed out, and a report came from the regiment with the order: SS-Hauptsturmführer Wolter is to reconnoiter transfer possibilities at Elbeuf for the remainder of the regiment and ferry over the I. Bataillon and remainder of the regiment. Wolter immediately set off with Münzenmaier on the B-Krad. We still had to handle collecting stragglers and arranging Funktrupps and Fernsprechtrupps.

I received the report from Münzenmaier in the presence of SS-Untersturmführer Stadler and personally delivered to SS-Obersturmbannführer Schultze (also referred to as 'the last Prussian' or 'the iron Gustav' – likely from his time with the II./'Germania' in 1935-1938), whereupon the order was issued to march to Rouen. Because I knew both 40-ton ferries at Couronne, I drove with the remainder of the regiment there and sent over 35 Schützenpanzerwagen, three of five 8-ton tractor units and 30 trucks. Sepp Dietrich and Heinz Harmel assigned us the marching route on the ferry St. Albert – Mons – Hasseelt – Venlo – Arnhem – Deventer – Diepenveen. Our battalion assembled there.

In St. Abert a Kampfgruppe was formed under SS-Obersturmbannführer Schultze. But this group's life did not last long. The I-Trupp and Versorgungskompanie had to march off already until 20:00 hours. The Allies had an easy game – we were without heavy weapons – 8.8 cm Kampfwagenkanone was the heaviest weapon. Schultze fell – the majority of the Kampfgruppe was taken into British captivity.

SS-Sturmbannführer Laubscheer was appointed Regimentsführer – we then received SS-Hauptsturmführer Lohr from Munich as the new Bataillonskommandeur."

Another member of the division recalls the retreat toward the Netherlands:

"At Mondidier – Hitler received the EK 1 here in World War I – the company had to form a Sperrverband. Then we continued over Peronne, where our quarters were in autumn 1943. We took positions once more at Bapaume. Our VW had a flat tire, and we lost sight of the company. Through Cambrai – Valenciennes – Tournai we reached Brussels. We, the driver of the VW and I, were greeted by the Belgians with flowers that were still potted. In Hasselt we were fired at by partisans of the white Brigade.

There were no losses. Behind Hasselt, our Schirrmeister, *inspected a Bianci with a trailer that was left behind. The vehicle was loaded with sacks of coffee, pepper, tobacco products, canned goods, etc. We first learned here that for provisions, there were also cans with chicken, delicious soups, etc.*

The truck's cooler had bullet holes. Suitable branches closed them. Through Aachen, we were stayed the night, we went through Gulpen to Deventer, where we moved into quarters. Under the command of SS-Obersturmführer *Baumgärtel our company was involved in the battles in Arnhem."*

Retreat from France

Conflicts in the Netherlands
(Arnhem-Nijmegen Region)

On 10 September 1944 the OKW ordered that a division of the II. *SS-Panzer-Korps* be replenished near the front, and the other at the homeland war area. Because the 10. *SS-Panzer-Division* "Frundsberg" was stronger than the 9. *SS-Panzer-Division* "Hohenstaufen" due to the supply of the *SS-Panzer-Jäger-Abteilung* 10 (27 *Jagdpanzer* IV under the command of *SS-Hauptsturmführer* Roestel), as well as the I. (Panther)/*SS-Panzer-Regiment* 10, the commanding general of the *II. SS-Panzer-Korps*, *SS-Obergruppenführer* and *General der Waffen-SS* Bittrich, decided to leave the 10. *SS-Panzer-Division* "Frundsberg" in the Arnhem region and continue to reinforce it with the 9. *SS-Panzer-Division* "Hohenstaufen," which was to be removed to the Reich.

With the detachment of the 9. *SS-Panzer-Division* "Hohenstaufen," it concerned *SS-Bataillon* "Segler" (sections of the *SS-Panzer-Grenadier-Regiment* 19) temporarily deployed within the framework of the 7. *Armee*, the *SS-Bataillon* "Euling," as well as a section of the *SS-Panzer-Artillerie-Regiment* 9 with two batteries of light *Feldhaubitzen* 10.5 cm (mot. Z.).

On 16 September 1944 *SS-Brigadeführer* and *Generalmajor* Harmel traveled to Bad Saarow in order to discuss the reformation of the 10. *SS-Panzer-Division* "Frundsberg" in the *SS-Führungshauptamt*, which was evacuated from Berlin. The commander of the *SS-Panzer-Regiment* 10, *SS-Obersturmbannführer* Paetsch, took over acting command of the division.

While already the first units as *SS-Kampfgruppe* "Heinke" arrived for front deployment, the remaining approximate 3,500 men occupied the following regions:

Divisionsstab and II./*SS-Panzer-Grenadier-Regiment* 22	Ruurlo
SS-Bataillon "Trapp" (sections of the *SS-Panzer-Grenadier-Regiment* 21)	Deventer
SS-Bataillon "Euling" (new I./*SS-Panzer-Grenadier-Regiment* 22)	Rheden
II./*SS-Panzer-Regiment* 10 (approximately 16 Panzer IV and *Sturmgeschütze*)	Vorden
Remainder/*SS-Panzer-Artillerie-Regiment* 10	Dieven
Remainder/*SS-Panzer-Aufklärungs-Abteilung* 10	Borcule
SS-Panzer-Nachrichten-Abteilung 10	Ruurlo

The enormous losses of the German *Wehrmacht* on all fronts in the summer of 1944 also led to great personnel difficulties in the *Waffen-SS*. In 1941, in the course of the rapid increase of the armed SS units, the *Führer* and *Unterführer* offices could often only be

Quarters of the 10. *SS-Panzer-Division* "Frundsberg."

Deployment of the *SS-Kampfgruppe* "Heinke" at the Neerpelt Bridgehead.

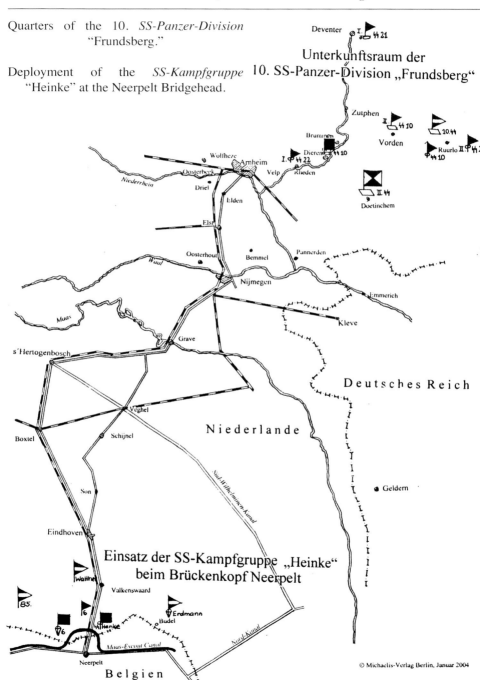

Unterkunftsraum der
10. SS-Panzer-Division „Frundsberg"

Einsatz der SS-Kampfgruppe „Heinke" beim Brückenkopf Neerpelt

© Michaelis-Verlag Berlin, Januar 2004

occupied improvisationally; the necessary men were lacking for the approximate required strength of the units. At this time the battalions of the 10. *SS-Panzer-Division* had, for example, only over approximately 20% of the required strength at their disposal! In October 1944 primarily members of the *Luftwaffe* were detached to the *Waffen-SS* on a large scale. A former member recalls:

"I was a Flugzeugführer, *and when the* Luftwaffe *no longer had fuel, we flyers were detached to* Felddivisionen. *So in late summer 1944 I came to the 10.* SS-Panzer-Division *'Frundsberg' as a so-called 'Hermann-Görung-Spende.'"*

Concerning this matter, the commander of the *SS-Feld-Ersatz-Bataillon 10* recalls:

"In mid-October 1944 I received the assignment of taking over the Feld-Ersatz-Bataillon *in Goor. This assignment was not what I imagined, and I was peeved for a moment. I perceived the order as a disciplinary transfer. In Goor I reached an agreement with the* SS-Sturmbannführer *present there, that he would maintain the training of the replacements and he would provide me only a few good trainers. The strength of the* Feld-Ersatz-Bataillon *at this time amounted to roughly 150-200 men. But nearly daily smaller troops arrived from the replacement units and military hospitals. A few days later roughly 1,500* Luftwaffe *members stood in front of me – from* Hauptfeldwebel *to* Gefreiten.*

Around a third of them came as technical personnel to the Werkstatt-Kompanien. *Roughly 200 men were taken as radio or telephone operators. Approximately 180 soldiers, who had already served as trainers, were used for* Unterführer *training. The remainder immediately went to the* Feld-Ersatz-Bataillon *for training.*

The key course elements were:

Shooting from the hip with the MG with live ammunition while walking and running. Throwing hand grenades with live hand grenades. Tank combat with Panzerfäuste. *Wagons of a* Feldbahn *– moved by a cable control – acted as enemy tanks.*

The units not used always acted as spectators. It is noteworthy how they crowded around to have their turn.

Finally 1,500 Russians came [ethnic Germans from Romania,[25] author's note] *– certainly it was the work of our 'Reichsheinis' to send these people to us. I felt sorry for them."*

---

25 A total of roughly 4,000 ethnic Germans served in the 10. *SS-Panzer-Division* "Frundsberg." Compare Appendix 6.

SS-Kampfgruppe "Heinke"

Without a real possibility of replenishing his division, *SS-Brigadeführer* and *General der Waffen-SS* Harmel already sent a *Kampfgruppe* to the front again on 13/14 September 1944. The British Guards Armored Division had formed a bridgehead over the Maas-Schelde Canal at Neerpelt on 12 September 1944. The German 1. *Fallschirm-Armee* located there immediately put all of its available strength into position for a counterthrust. This was primarily the *Fallschirmjäger-Regiment* "Hoffmann" formed from ground crew of the *Luftwaffe* and inexperienced in war, as well as the *Fallschirmjäger-Regiment* 6 under the command of *Oberstleutnant* von der Heydte. Because these forces would not be sufficient to crush the enemy bridgehead, the *Heeresgruppe* "B" had ordered the deployment of a *Kampfgruppe* of the 10. *SS-Panzer-Division* "Frundsberg."

Under the commander of the *SS-Feld-Ersatz-Bataillon* 10, *SS-Sturmbannführer* Heinke, the following transferred into the threatened region and were placed under the command of *Oberst* Walther[26]:

- *SS-Bataillon* "Segler" (assigned sections of the *SS-Pz.-Grenadier-Regiment* 19)
- *SS-Bataillon* "Richter" (sections of the *SS-Panzer-Grenadier-Regiment* 21)
- a *Kompanie/SS-Panzer-Aufklärungs-Abteilung* 10
- a *Kompanie/SS-Panzer-Pionier-Bataillon* 10
- a battery/*SS-Panzer-Artillerie-Regiment* 10 (six *Panzerhaubitzen*)
- a *Kompanie/SS-Panzer-Jäger-Abteilung* 10 (15 *Sturmgeschütze* IV)

The former commander of the *Fallschirmjäger-Regiment* 4 was assigned with the annihilation of the Neerpelt bridgehead from the 1. *Fallschirm-Armee*, and with this took over the command of:

- the *Fallschirmjäger-Regiment* "Hoffmann"
- the *Fallschirmjäger-Regiment* 6
- The *Luftwaffen-Strafbataillon* 6
- The *SS-Kampfgruppe* "Heinke"

The left neighbor of the *Kampfgruppe* "Walther" (strength: approximately 3,000 men) was the *Fallschirmjäger-Division* "Erdmann," the right neighbor the 85. *Infanterie-Division*.

The German attack began in the morning hours of 15 September 1944 and remained under heavy losses without artillery support within English resistance, as well as the swampy ground. The next day the *Heeresgruppe* "B" ordered the continuation of the attack,

---

26 Erich Walther was awarded the Knight's Cross on 24 May 1940 as Major and commander of the I./ *Fallschirmjäger-Regiment* 1. On 2 March 1944 he received the 411. Oak Leaves and on 1 February 1945 the 131. Swords to the Knight's Cross of the Iron Cross.

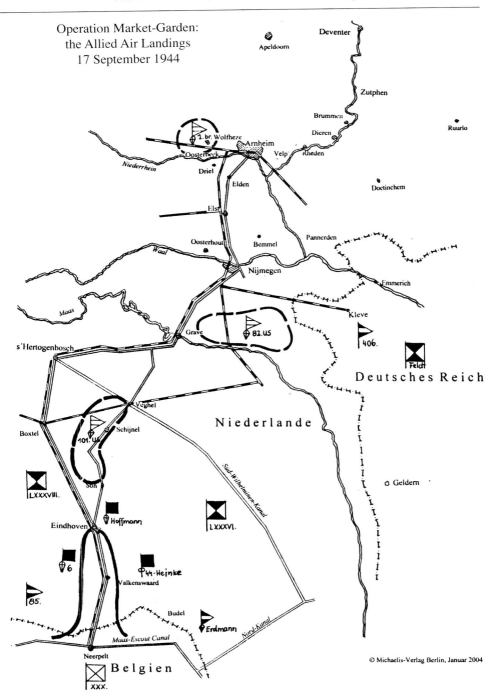

Operation Market-Garden:
the Allied Air Landings
17 September 1944

Deventer

Apeldoorn

Zutphen

Brummen

Ruurlo

Dieren

1. br. Wolfheze

Arnheim

Oosterbeek

Velp

Rheden

Niederrhein

Driel

Elden

Doetinchem

Elst

Oosterhout

Bemmel

Pannerden

Waal

Nijmegen

Emmerich

Maas

Grave

Kleve

82. US

406.

s'Hertogenbosch

Feldt

Deutsches Reich

Veghel

Niederlande

Boxtel

Schijnel

101. US

Zuid-Willhelminen-Kanal

Son

ⓞ Geldern

LXXXVIII.

Hoffmann

LXXXVI.

Eindhoven

6

44-Heinke

Valkenswaard

85.

Budel

Erdmann

Nord-Kanal

Maas-Escout Canal

Neerpelt

© Michaelis-Verlag Berlin, Januar 2004

Belgien

XXX.

but due to the British air superiority and superiority of heavy weapons (tanks and artillery) the operation remained a hopeless undertaking. Therefore, the bold *Oberst* Walther ordered only localized action, and ordered moreso the development of defense positions at the bridgehead. He knew that a large-scale British offensive was to be dealt with shortly.

Sooner than expected, it had already begun by 17 September 1944. Around 14:00 hours heavy artillery fire on the bridgehead began. Among others, most of the six *Panzerhaubitzen* of the *SS-Kampfgruppe* "Heinke" became unfit for action. Roughly an hour later strong armed forces from the bridgehead attacked the *Kampfgruppe* "Walther" head on. The British were able to break through in the area between the *Fallschirmjäger-Regiment* "Hoffmann" and the *Fallschirmjäger-Regiment* 6, as well as between the *Fallschirmjäger-Regiment* 6 and the 85. *Infanterie Division* (*Kampfgruppe* "Chill") and advance on Valkenswaard.

While the *SS-Bataillon* "Segler" attempted to maintain contact with the *Fallschirmjäger-Regiment* "Hoffmann," the *SS-Bataillon* "Richter," along with sections of the *Fallschirmjäger-Division* "Erdmann" were pushed back to Budel and encircled there. After *Panzerfaust* firing from four Sherman-Panzer, the rest of the battalion (approximately 100 men) were able to retreat to Weert. *SS-Hauptsturmführer* Roestel was able to intercept the British tank advance toward Eindhoven for a short time with his eight remaining *Sturmgeschütze* IV in front of Valkenswaard.

The British offensive of the XXX Corps left the German front around the bridgehead battered. East of the breakthrough, primarily the units of the *SS-Kampfgruppe* "Heinke" within the framework of the LXXXVI. *Armee-Korps* (*General der Infanterie* Obstfelder[27]) attempted to maintain the main front—to the west was the *Fallschirmjäger-Regiment* 6, sections of the 85. *Infanterie-Division* (*Generalleutnant* Chill[28]), as well as the *Fallschirmjäger-Regiment* "Hoffmann" within the framework of the LXXXVIII. *Armee-Korps* (*General der Infanterie* Reinhard[29]). *Oberst* Hoffmann was assigned with the defense of Eindhoven—which was not feasible with the available troops!

On 18 September 1944 around 19:00 hours the British Guards Armored Division reached sections of the American 101ˢᵗ Airborne Division, which jumped north of Eindhoven. Attempts to stop the quick advance of the British XXX Corps over Schijndel to Grave by flank attacks of the newly supplied 59. *Infanterie-Division* from the west, as well as the *Panzer-Brigade* 107 from the east, remained unsuccessful.

---

27 See Appendix 7
28 See Appendix 7
29 See Appendix 7

Bridge at Grave.

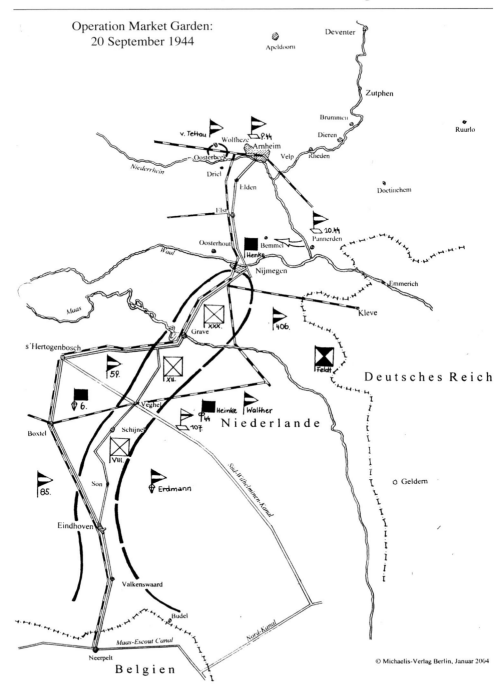

Operation Market Garden:
20 September 1944

© Michaelis-Verlag Berlin, Januar 2004

On 23 September 1944 sections of the *Kampfgruppe* "Walther" (assembled in the Gemert region), including the *SS-Kampfgruppe* "Heinke," attacked the Allied troops at Vegehl in order to cut the units advancing on Nijmegen from the lines of communication. Here there was also no success. Due to the development of the situation, on 26 September 1944 the German command ordered the retreat of the *Kampfgruppen* to the south to the Maas, and finally behind the Waal. The remainder of the *SS-Kampfgruppe* "Heinke" came under the command of the 10. *SS-Panzer-Division* "Frundsberg" again.

SS-Kampfgruppe "Brinkmann"

With the formation of the British bridgehead at Neerpelt on 12 September 1944, Field Marshal Montgomery considered a large-scale air-land operation. The 1ˢᵗ Allied Airborne Army (U.S. Lieutenant General Brereton), with three and a half airborne divisions (82ⁿᵈ, 101ˢᵗ U.S. Airborne Divisions, 1ˢᵗ British Airborne Division, and Polish 1ˢᵗ Independent Parachute Brigade), was to occupy the bridges at the Wilhelmina Canal, Maas, Waal, and Lower Rhine ("MARKET"), and keep free for the quickly advancing British XXX Corps (Guards Armored Division, 43ʳᵈ and 50ᵗʰ Infantry Divisions - "GARDEN"). Thereby, it was to be made possible for the British 2ⁿᵈ Army with the American airborne divisions to advance to Ijsselmeer, and thus maintain favorable lines of departure for the invasion of the Ruhr area. With the shutdown of the German heavy industry the war would be ended within a short period of time.

The Commander-in-Chief of the Allied forces in Europe, General Eisenhower, agreed to Field Marshal Montgomery's suggestions after initial hesitation, and on 17 September 1944 the greatest air landing of World War II occurred: Operation Market Garden.

The British 1ˢᵗ Airborne Division (General Urquhart) landed—due to the lack of an alternative—west of Arnhem with the objective of occupying the bridge over the Lower Rhine. The American 82ⁿᵈ Airborne Division (General Gavin) landed in the Nijmwegen region, in order to capture the bridges over the Waal and the Maas (at Grave), and the American 101ˢᵗ Airborne Division (General Taylor) was to occupy the bridges in the Son – St. Oedenrode region and Veghel (Wilhelmina Canal).

The first wave of the British 1ˢᵗ Airborne Division consisted of the 1ˢᵗ Airborne Brigade, which was supposed to secure the landing area around Wolfheze, as well as the 1ˢᵗ Independent Parachute Brigade, which was to occupy the main street in Arnhem, as well as the bridges. A short time later the I and III/1ˢᵗ Independent Parachute Brigade was involved in combat with the *Kampfgruppe* "Weber" (IV./*Luftnachrichten-Regiment* 213), as well as *SS-Panzer-Grenadier-Ausbildungs- und Ersatz-Bataillon* 16 (SS-*Hauptsturmführer* Krafft), and the II. *Bataillon* was able to advance without great resistance. The occupation of the railroad bridge somewhat outside of Arnhem was unsuccessful; German combat engineers detonated the bridge before the British paratroopers were able to take possession of it. They reoriented themselves immediately and marched on the road bridge in Arnhem.

Roughly half an hour later, after the first air landings, the commanding general of the II. *SS-Panzer-Korps* was informed of the British operation. *SS-Obergruppenführer* and *General der Waffen-SS* immediately informed the remainder of both *SS-Panzer-Divisionen* under him. The 9. *SS-Panzer-Division* "Hohenstaufen" was to immediately stop the loading to Germany. While the majority of the division was to annihilate the British air landing west of Arnhem, the motorized *SS-Panzer-Aufklärungs-Abteilung* 9 (*SS-Hauptsturmführer* Gräbner) was to advance to Nijmegen with approximately 30 *Schützenpanzerwagen* and secure the bridges over the Waal. The 10. *SS-Panzer-Division* "Frundsberg" received the order to follow the *SS-Panzer-Aufklärungs-Abteilung* 9 to Nijmwegen and occupy a bridgehead position there. For the *SS-Panzer-Aufklärungs-Abteilung* 9, under the tactical command of the 10. *SS-Panzer-Division* "Frundsberg" in the Nijmegen region, the *SS-Panzer-Aufklärungs-Abteilung* 10 (*SS-Sturmbannführer* Brinkmann) available somewhat later was supplied to the 9. *SS-Panzer-Division* "Hohenstaufen."

The first assignment of the *SS-Kampfgruppe* "Brinkmann" was to secure the road bridge in Arnhem. The first battles took place around 20:00 hours with sections of the II./1. *Fallschirmjäger-Brigade* that just occupied the bridge! As more sections of the 10. *SS-Panzer-Division* "Frundsberg" (among others, the I./SS-*Panzer-Grenadier-Regiment* 22) reached the bridge, in order to comply with the order to march to Nijmegen, they were surprised that the bridge was under heavy British fire. While *SS-Sturmbannführer* Brinkmann received the assignment to fight to free the bridge again, the other units received the order to evade toward Pannerden. Here the *SS-Panzer-Pionier-Bataillon* 10 was to cross the river.

During the night of 17 September 1944 the *SS-Kampfgruppe* "Brinkmann" unsuccessfully attacked. The British paratroopers under the command of Lieutenant Colonel Frost had entrenched themselves in the houses west of the bridge, and thereby had good possibilities for defense. On the morning of 18 September 1944 *SS-Brigadeführer* and *Generalmajor der Waffen-SS* Harmel, alarmed the day before in Bad Saarow, arrived in Arnhem and took command of the road bridge up to and including Nijmegen. As a result, the reinforced *SS-Panzer-Aufklärungs-Abteilung* 10 again came under the command of the 10. *SS-Panzer-Division* "Frundsberg."

On 18 September 1944 the *SS-Kampfgruppe* "Brinkmann" was reinforced by the *Kampfgruppe* "Knaust." This was formed as the so-called "Gneisenau"-*Einheit* from the *Panzer-Grenadier-Ersatz- und Ausbildungs-Bataillonen* 16 and 57, and consisted of four *Panzer-Grenadier-Kompanien* and one *Panzer-Jäger-Kompanie* (strength: barely 700 men). The *Kampfgruppe* "Knaust" initially relieved the *SS-Bataillon* "Euling" that was still in the area of the bridge so that they could likewise march to Pannerden. On 18 September 1944 the German *Wehrmachtbericht* reported:

"In the Dutch region the enemy dropped paratroopers and airborne troops behind our front in the Arnhem, Nimwegen, and Eindhoven region yesterday afternoon after previous heavy air attacks. During the afternoon the enemy then arrived between Antwerp and Maastricht for combat in order to make contact with his units that jumped. Especially in the Neerpelt region, heavy combat developed during which the enemy was able to gain territory toward the north. Concentric counterattacks have begun against the enemy airborne forces."

While the *SS-Kampfgruppe* "Brinkmann" initially tried in vain to fight the British paratroopers in the region of the northern bridge ramp, *SS-Hauptsturmführer* Gräbner ordered his *SS-Panzer-Aufklärungs-Abteilung* 9 to drive to Arnhem and fight free the bridge from the south—a plan that went against the expressed order to secure Nijmegen—and finally claimed a roughly 60% loss of man and materiel. *SS-Hauptsturmführer* Gräbner fell in this stubborn act, for which he presumably would have received the Oak Leaves to the Knight's Cross if it had succeeded.

After the British attempt—reinforced by further landings of troops—to relieve the Parachute Battalion "Frost" at the bridge had failed—on 20 September 1944 the *SS-Kampfgruppe* "Brinkmann" continued the attack from the region of the freight depot and the factory building east of the bridge ramp. Flame-throwers, combat engineer explosives, and *Panzerfäuste* were used, and each house overpowered. When on the next day the resistance of the Battalion "Frost" subsided, the bridge was again passable for the German troops.

Bataillon "Knaust" subsequently transferred with the eight tanks and *Sturmgeschütze*—placed under their command by the *Panzer-Ersatz- und Ausbildungs-Abteilung* 17 the day before—over the Rhine bridge into the Elst region, in order to reinforce the struggling troops of the 10. *SS-Panzer-Division* "Frundsberg."

At the same time, on 21 September 1944 a Polish parachute brigade landed at Driel in order to reinforce the British troops, which in the meantime were encircled in the Oosterbeek region, until the arrival of the XXX Corps. While the British 43ʳᵈ Infantry

Division advanced from the south into the Driel region in order to make contact with the Polish allies, sections of the *SS-Kampfgruppe* "Brinkmann" attempted to prevent contact between the British paratroopers at Oosterbeek and the greatly depleted Polish troops already approaching over the Lower Rhine.

During the intense battles at Oosterbeek there was a unique occurrence. After intercepting the enemy radio the 9. *SS-Panzer-Division* "Hohenstaufen" offered the British troops to take their wounded. Between 22 and 24 September 1944 a total of roughly 2,200 British and Polish paratroopers were taken by the *SS-Sanitäts-Abteilung* 9 and brought to military hospitals and hospitals in and around Arnhem.

On 25 September 1944 the I./*SS-Panzer-Aufklärungs-Abteilung* 10 on the Lower Rhine, together with sections of the *Kampfgruppe/SS-Unterführerschule* Arnhem likewise deployed there successfully, fought sections of the Polish Parachute Brigade, as well as advance troops of the British 43rd Infantry Division. Furthermore, slightly north, German forces succeeded in dividing the Oosterbeek pocket. The next day the Commander-in-Chief of the British 2nd Army decided to give up positions for the planned bridgehead north of the Rhine at Oosterbeek, and to withdraw the remaining troops on the southern shore of the Rhine in the area of the XXX Corps. On 26 September 1944 2,100 members of the British 1st Airborne Division and the Polish Parachute Brigade were able to retreat over the Rhine to the lines of the British 43rd Infantry Division at Driel. The next day the *Wehrmachtbericht* reported:

"In the Arnhem region on 26 September the last resistance of the encircled 1st English Airborne Division was broken.

In the ten-day bitter combat the forces of all Wehrmachtteile *that quickly pulled together under the leadership of the commanding general of a* SS-Panzerkorps, SS-Obergruppenführer, *and* General der Waffen-SS *succeeded in completely destroying an English elite division despite the toughest resistance and reinforcement from continued air landings. All enemy attempts of relieving the encircled division from the south failed under heavy bloody losses. A total of 6,450 captives were brought in, thousands dead, 30* Panzerabwehrgeschütze, *further* Geschütze *and numerous weapons, and 250 motor vehicles captured. Furthermore, 1,000 transport gliders were destroyed or captured and over 100 aircraft shot down."*

After the end of the battles the *SS-Kampfgruppe* "Brinkmann" proceeded to the region of the 10. *SS-Panzer-Division* "Frundsberg" fighting at Elst.

Above: Briefing in Arnhem — 18 September 1944. Below: Alarmed, the *Panzer-Grenadier* reached the city partially by bicycle.

The Arnhem Bridge.

SS-Kampfgruppe "Reinhold"

On 17 September 1944 the American 82ⁿᵈ Airborne Division landed in the Nijmegen – Grave region, and was able to initially occupy the Maas bridge at Grave and a side canal bridge southwest of Nijmegen.

Completely surprised, the defense at Nijmegen from the German side had to be overhastily improvised. *Oberst* Henke was assigned with the formation of a *Kampfgruppe* and then led:

- 1 regiment of the *Fallschirmjäger-Ersatz- und Ausbildungs-Division*
- 3 companies of the *Landesschützen-Ersatz- und Ausbildungs-Bataillon* 6
- 1 company of the *Fallschirm-Panzer-Ers.- und Ausb.-Regiments* "Hermann Göring"

Oberst Henke—aware of the numerical superiority of the opponent—concentrated on the defense of the railway bridge and road bridge in the city. There was still no fighting, because the troops of the American 82ⁿᵈ Airborne Division focused on the strategically important hills southeast of Nijmegen. Here the Division z. b. V. 406, formed by the *Wehrkreiskommando* VI after the initiation of Operation "Walküre," stood ready for attack within the *Korps* "Feldt." After the hypothetical annihilation of the U.S. Division (sic!) and handing over of the region to the 10. *SS-Panzer-Division* "Frundsberg," the units of the WKK VI were to continue to advance south. A utopian concept, if one considers that these troops mostly consisted of old age groups (*Landesschütze*) and *Ersatz- und Ausbildungseinheiten* without any combat experience and heavy weapons!

On 18 September 1944 the *Division z. b. V.* 406 attacked the American 82ⁿᵈ Airborne Division in the Mook – Groesbeek region. After the U.S. paratroopers received reinforcement the attack came to a standstill. While the German units went back to the lines of departure and waited for reinforcement from sections of the 3. and 5. *Fallschirmjäger-Division*, *SS-Brigadeführer* and *Generalmajor der Waffen-SS* Harmel ordered the formation of a *Kampfgruppe* that was to advance to Nijmwegen.

Because the Arnhem bridge was still under fire from British paratroopers, *SS-Sturmbannführer* Reinhold (Kdr. II./SS-Panzer-Regiment 10) led the following to Pannerden:

- the II./*SS-Panzer-Regiment* 10
- the *SS-Bataillon* "Euling" (I./*SS-Panzer-Grenadier Regiment* 22)[30]
- the III./*SS-Panzer-Artillerie-Regiment* 10

---

30 The *SS-Bataillon* "Euling" was only just relieved by the *Kampfgruppe* "Knaust" in Arnhem.

There, on 18 September 1944 the *SS-Panzer-Pionier-Bataillon* 10 improvised the crossing of the river. The heavy weapons were transported by means of a 70-ton *Pontonfähre*. In the course of the day the *SS-* so-called *SS-Kampfgruppe* "Reinhold" reached Nijmwegen through Gendt and reinforced the *Kampfgruppe* "Henke" here.

The next day the British Guards Armored Division reached the American 82ⁿᵈ Airborne Division through Grave. The immediate attempt—supported by 40 tanks—to reach the road bridge over the Waal failed in the city center. Here the Allied troops suffered the same fate as the *SS-Panzer-Aufklärungs-Abteilung* 9 in Arnhem: the men of the *SS-Kampfgruppe* "Reinhold" entrenched themselves in the houses, and with *Panzerfäuste* knocked out numerous enemy tanks. Roughly 500 m in front of the objective the attack collapsed.

In order to avoid more heavy losses, American paratroopers set out west of the city in makeshift boats over the Waal in order to attack the German bridgehead in Nijmegen from the back from the north. The operation unsuccessfully proceeded with heavy losses. However, on 20 September 1944 the American-British forces succeeded in breaking through to the bridge in a second attempt with large artillery and tank deployment.

Because the bridgehead could no longer be held, the *Heeresgruppe* "B" authorized the retreat to the northern shore of the Waal. While on 19/20 September 1944 the majority of both *Kampfgruppen* "Henke" and "Reinhold" were able to escape the enemy, the *SS-Bataillon* "Euling" was encircled. Finally, only approximately 60 men succeeded in retreating over the Waal.

The *Kampfgruppe* "Henke" moved into positions at Fort "Hof van Holland" and the *SS-Kampfgruppe* "Reinhold" east of the railway bridge at Lent. Here they also reached the tanks of the II./SS-*Panzer-Regiment* 10, as well as sections of the *SS-Panzer-Grenadier-Regiment* 22. All deployed units of the 10. *SS-Panzer-Division* "Frundsberg" were thus under the command of *SS-Brigadeführer* and *Generalmajor der Waffen-SS* Harmel again.

Sign to Pannerden (above) and Dutch prewar bunker on the southern shore.

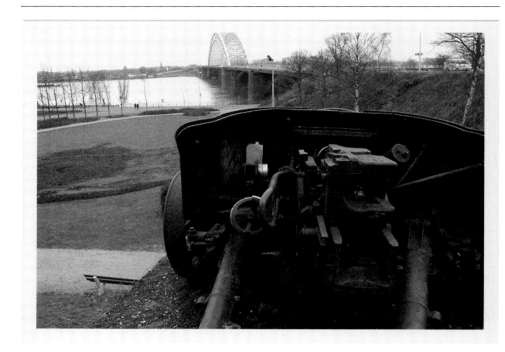

7.5 cm Pak/40 at the Nijmegen bridge.

Kampfgruppe/10. SS-Panzer-Division "Frundsberg"

After the retreat of the *Kampfgruppen* "Henke" and "Reinhold" the Allies immediately formed a bridgehead north of Nijmegen. To relieve the battered British 1ˢᵗ Airborne Division in the Oosterbeek region, the 1ˢᵗ Polish Parachute Brigade landed at Briel, and from the Nijmegen bridgehead the British 43ʳᵈ Infantry Division, among others, were on the offensive. The troops of the XXX Corps reached Elst on 21 September 1944; thus, they separated roughly six kilometers from their comrades encircled behind the Lower Rhine.

In order to intercept the enemy advance on Arnhem the *Sperrverband* "Harzer" (commander: *SS-Obersturmbannführer* Harzer) was formed of:

- *Kampfgruppe* "Schoerken"
- *Kampfgruppe* "Koehnen" (*Marine-Kampfgruppe* 642)
- *Luftwaffe-Bataillon* "Kauer"
- *Festungs-Maschinengewehr-Bataillon* 47
- *III./Landstorm* "Nederland"[31]

and led from Arnhem toward Elst.

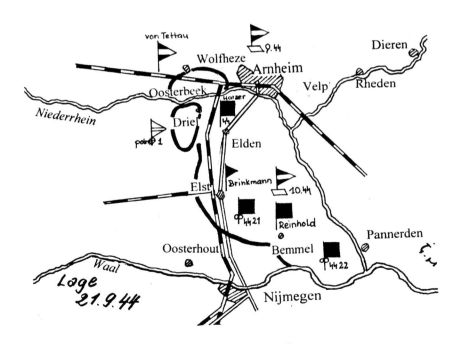

---

31 For this history of the *Landstorm* "Nederland" see Michaelis, Rolf: *Die Grenadier-Division der Waffen-SS*, Erlangen 1995.

The *10. SS-Panzer-Division*—due to the meager strength (the units still had only roughly 20-25% of the required strength) referred to as *Kampfgruppe/10. SS-Panzer-Division* "Frundsberg"—moved into the Elst – Bemmel – Waal line. Sections of the *SS-Panzer-Grenadier-Regiment* 22 formed the left flank from the Waal to Bemmel. It connected to the *SS-Kampfgruppe* "Reinhold" north of Bemmel, and there were sections of the *SS-Panzer-Grenadier-Regiment* to Elst. At Elst the *Kampfgruppe/10. SS-Panzer-Division* "Frundsberg" made contact with the *III./Landstorm* "Nederland," which was reinforced by sections of the *Bataillon* "Knaust."

Attempts to hit the northward advancing enemy in the flanks had to be unsuccessfully stopped—on the contrary, due to the heavy enemy pressure on 25 September 1944 positions at Elst had to be abandoned and set back to a line south of Elden.

One day later the fate of the British 1ˢᵗ Airborne Division was sealed; they gave up the battle, and the remainder tried to save themselves over the Lower Rhine to the south. There was again a large advance of the XXX Corps toward the northwest! In heavy resistance combat the German troops of *Sperrgruppe* "Harzer," as well as the *Kampfgruppe/10. SS-Panzer-Division* "Frundsberg," were able to maintain the main front and force back the opponent even farther.

The *Oberbefehlshaber* of *Heeresgruppe* "B," *Generalfeldmarschall* Model, ordered *SS-Obergruppenführer* and *General der Waffen-SS* Bittrich to immediately work out an offensive with which the narrow bridgehead over the Waal could be annihilated and a continuous main front could be formed along the river. In the forefront of this attack the railway bridge, as well as the road bridge in Nijmegen, were at least partially damaged by German *Kampfflieger* and *Kampfschwimmer* so that the Allied reinforcements would be impeded. However, a complete annihilation was unsuccessful.

On 1 October 1944 the II. *SS-Panzer-Korps*, reinforced by numerous *Wehrmacht* units (among others, *Kampfgruppen* of the 9. and 116. *Panzer-Division*), mustered for attack. The *Kampfgruppe/9. Panzer-Division* was to advance on Elst, the *Kampfgruppe/10. SS-Panzer-Division* "Frundsberg" on Bemmel, and the 116. *Panzer-Division* on Driel. The *Wehrmachtbericht* reported:

"*Angriffsgruppen of the Army and the* Waffen-SS *broke into British positions between the Lower Rhine and the Waal and threw back the fighting opponent to the west.*"

During combat the *Kampfgruppe/10. SS-Panzer-Division* "Frundsberg" suffered the greatest losses since the beginning of fighting in the Netherlands on 4 October 1944 in enemy resistance fire. While the 9. and 116. *Panzer-Division* continued their attack, the next day the *Kampfgruppe*/10. *SS-Panzer-Division* had to move into defense at the Linge Canal. As a result of the enemy resistance the offensive against the allied bridgehead remained unfinished, and completely ceased on 7 October 1944. The then *SS-Rottenführer* Karl Schneider (I./*SS-Panzer-Grenadier-Regiment* 21) recalls:

"On 19 July 1925 I was born in Rheinbischofsheim (Kreis Kehl) and was called up on 5 October 1942 to the RAD-Feld-Abteilung K *1/322 (military postal service number 19 573) to Lubeln/Westmark. After action in southern France (Camarquel Bay of Biscay) and the Saar region, in April 1943 the discharge to Karlsruhe followed. Here I enlisted for the 4./*Grenadier-Ausbildungs- und Ersatz-Bataillon *111 and arrived on the eastern front in December 1943 in the region south of Mogilew. In the 4./*Grenadier-Regiment *111 of the 35.* Infanterie-Division *(Fisch-Division) I was east of the Dnieper, and as of the beginning of January 1944 deployed in the Pinsk Marshes (approximately 30 km south of Bobruisk).*

On 2 March 1944 I had shrapnel in my left foot and initially came into the Minsk military hospital, then the Thorn field hospital, and finally to the Brussels reserve military hospital. From there in mid-June 1944I went to the Genesenden-Kompanie des Grenadier-Ersatz-Bataillon *111 to Vlissingen/Walcheren.*

When the Allies advanced from Normandy our company (Chief: Oberleutnant Gebauer*), along with other troops were deployed west of Antwerp against British tanks at the beginning of August 1944 and at Beveren nearly completely annihilated.*

On 26 August 1944, while crossing over the Waal with a ferry at Gorinchem, as a straggler I joined the SS-Panzer-Grenadier-Ersatz- und Ausbildungs-Bataillon *4. My previous rank was crossed out in the pay book and replaced by* SS-Rottenführer—*it was that simple to become a soldier of the* Waffen-SS!

During the battles in Oosterbeek I came to the 9. SS-Panzer-Division *'Hohenstaufen,' and on 1 October 1944 as driver of a* Schützenpanzerwagen *was transferred to the 1./* SS-Panzer-Grenadier-Regiment *21. Shortly after my arrival the 1.* Kompanie *under SS-* Untersturmführer *Haase mustered for the attack through Heuvel toward Elst. The attack remained under heavy resistance fire. During the following night a British patrol invaded Heuvel, but was noticed by us and fought off. On 2 October 1944 the English formed up for the assault. The* main front *could only be held with great effort. On the night of 3 October 1944 our company, forming from the Baal region, was able to again fight free the road junction south of Heuvel. In doing so, a number of English were taken into captivity.*

But the British did not let up. After we were forced to give up Haalderen, on 6 October 1944 we went into a new defense position on the Linge Canal. The entire front sector between the Lower Rhine and the Waal was only occupied as a base."

Karl Schneider

Karl Schneider (right) in the *RAD-Feld-Abt. K 1/322.*

Astonishingly Hitler, contrary to his other *Haltbefehl*, authorized to take back the main front behind the Lower Rhine: on 8/9 October 1944 initially the 116. *Panzer-Division* was released from the front, and until 14 October 1944 the *Kampfgruppen* of the 9. *Panzer-* and 10. *SS-Panzer-Division* "Frundsberg." In the sector of the unit (Arnhem – Millingen), at times also referred to as *SS-Kampfgruppe* "Harmel," however, smaller bridgeheads were maintained at the Arnhem bridge, east of Huissen, and Angeren, as well as at Pannerden.

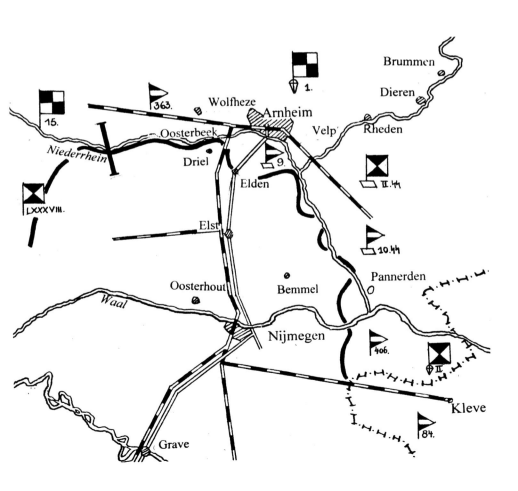

While the front in this sector calmed down, towards the west there was further combat with the LXXXVIII. *Armee-Korps*, during the course of which a *Kampfgruppe* was formed and deployed from a battalion of the *SS-Panzer-Grenadier-Regimenter* 21 and 22 under the command of *SS-Obersturmbannführer* Traupe. In the Arnhem area there were primarily localized operations. The then *SS-Rottenführer* Karl Schneider (1./*SS-Panzer-Grenadier-Regiment* 21) recalls an incident that led to a report to the Red Cross in Geneva:

"On 1 November 1944 I volunteered for a patrol operation that was to reconnoiter from the Doornenburg base toward Haalderen. Along with an Unterscharführer *and* six Grenadiere *we were assigned to reconnoiter the positions and troop strength of the opponent. From there, the British repeatedly tried to attack our bases and throw us over the Lower Rhine in the last days. Our positions, partially in the water or marshy meadow area, were raked with gunfire the entire day from enemy artillery of all calibers. When our patrol, then south of Fliern, unexpectedly came upon a British position approximately 1 km east of Haalderen, we were forced to retreat by heavy sMG fire and* Granatwerfer *fire. During this armed attack one of our men was severely injured on his leg, whereby he was unable to bring himself under secure cover. From a position approximately 150 m from our wounded comrade we heard his cry for help. His leg was torn up, and we needed to get him, otherwise he would have certainly bled to death.*

We then decided with four men, unarmed, without a belt and without a helmet, to rescue our severely injured comrade. We had obtained a Red Cross flag in the hopes that the Englanders would acknowledge it. Two Grenadiere *carried the stretcher, and the* Unterscharführer *called the opponent posts that were recognizably roughly 50 m away in their positions. It was a clear and light night. We were just getting ready to lay the severely injured comrade on the stretcher when fire was opened on us from submachine guns. Leaving behind our comrade we jumped under cover, and the* Unterscharführer's *arm was grazed. But our comrade was bleeding to death between the positions!*

When we arrived back at Doornenburg we reported this incident, which was passed along to the II. SS-Panzer-Korps. The printing of a leaflet was arranged, that on 3 November 1944 there were shots from the Pannerden region into the opposing positions at Haalderen."

This leaflet was started by *SS-Obergruppenführer* and *General der Waffen-SS* Bittrich, and read:

"*27 October – 6:00 hours – north of Elst:* Major *Rabbidge and* Leutnant *Twist were captured by the VII. Green Howards by one of my* Spähtrupps. *One or two of their men, who coincidentally were with both of these officers, were wounded and brought back to their lines by their stretcher bearers, who, unarmed, waved a Red Cross Flag.*

My people who stood by, of course, did not prevent them, and thereby very likely saved the life of the wounded and helpless soldier.

1. November 1944 – 20:00 hours – east of Haalderen: four of my men – they were unarmed without helmet or belt – a Red Cross flag waving and on the way to pick up one of my soldiers, who a short time before was wounded during a patrol. My people were there to pick up the wounded when fire was opened on them and, leaving the wounded and helpless soldier, had to jump back.

As of today: If I find out of such an incident, like that on 1 November 1944, I will give the order to open fire on unarmored stretcher bearers, even if they wave a Red Cross flag. I cannot believe that British officers want to ruin their good reputation as 'Gentlemen' by issuing orders to open fire on unarmored stretcher bearers, which certainly would not be considered 'fair play' on both sides."

The former commander of the *SS-Panzer-Pionier-Bataillon* 10 recalls the missions of his battalion in the Arnhem – Millingen region:

"*Before the air landing of the 1ˢᵗ English Airborne Division demanded deployment we had pulled together for replenishment. My* Pionier-Bataillon *consisted by now of two battered companies. Through the disbandment of the 1. armored* Pionier-Kompanie, *the* Pionierzug *and the* Stabskompanie *I first filled a* Pionier-Kompanie *(mot.) ready for action under the* Kompanieführer *Baumgärtel. After a reorganization as well as replacements, I formed a second* Pionier-Kompanie *(mot.) under* Kompanieführer *Munski.*

I had to deliver this company to a unit deployed to the right of us for minesweeping. Baumgärtel and I were then the first at the Nijmegen bridge with a Grenadier-Bataillon *during the air landing alarm. Baumgärtel remained there in action until the conclusion, and nearly all replacements were supplied to him. One regiment had its command post in a type of castle with a tower that we often used as an observational point.*

I was often in the region of both regiments – one of the regiment commanders had newly arrived to the division. Mines were often transferred, and temporary fortifications due to the terrain. The ferries made much work for us because we could only use the listed ferries; the Lower Rhine had a stone wall bank reinforcement. The church spires also had to be detonated because it would attract artillery fire to us like precision fire. Baumgärtel was awarded with the German Cross in Gold. He later fell at Stettin [today Szczecin in Poland].

On the Lower Rhine a position was expanded, but that, however, had no effect. At the far right of the sector comrade Roestel was deployed and had established an observation point in a brickyard smoke stack, which was then constantly under artillery fire. Eventually, we detonated the smoke stack. A clear field of fire also had to be created. Therefore, an old Dutch concrete bunker had to be detonated. At the ferries we had several 2 cm and 3.7 cm Flak. Often the dikes that were hit by artillery and fighter-bombers had to be restored.

During loading, with the remainder of my Stabskompanie and all other available men I had to repel an attack in a wooded area, in which 6 Panther-Panzer also took part. Later I was relieved by a Landesschützen-Regiment. I still remember that at that time a special order of the division was issued, in which my battalion and I were named."

Though November 1944 in the Aachen region an American offensive was looming, the 10. SS-Panzer-Division "Frundsberg" received the transfer order as *Heeresgruppenreserve* to the south. In the then calm combat sector of Arnhem – Millingen a *Panzer-Division* was dispensable in the positions! The *Oberbefehlshaber* of the 1. *Fallschirm-Armee*, *Generaloberst* Student, left the men in an order of the day on 18 November 1944:

"On 18 November 1944 the 10. SS-Panzer-Division 'Frundsberg' leaves the area of the Fallschirm-Armee.

Under the circumspect and decisive leadership of their commander the division has made exceptional achievements in attack and defense in constant action since 21 September 1944 and fulfilled all of the tasks presented to them in exemplary bravery. The division took special part in the difficult battles from 17-26 September 1944 that led to the complete destruction of the 1ˢᵗ English Airborne Division. I give special recognition to all Führer, Unterführer, and Mannschaften, and wish the division success and soldier's fortune for all further assignments.

I am certain that the Division 'Frundsberg' will contribute to the final vvictory of our people.

Long live the Führer!"

Positions at the Arnhem – Millingen line.

Positions at the Arnhem – Millingen line.

SS-Kampfgruppe "Traupe"

Although the British 2ⁿᵈ Army did not reach their ambitious objective of Operation "Market Garden" to form a bridgehead over the Lower Rhine at Arnhem, Allied troops were at a loss until shortly in front of Arnhem. In order to face—even if moreso theoretical—the flank threat on 24 October 1944 the British troops began with an offensive in the Turnhout – Tilburg – s'Hertogenbosch region.

The German 15. *Armee* here could not withstand the concentrated onslaught, and already on the first day requested the support of the 1. *Fallschirm-Armee*. They issued the order to the II. *SS-Panzer-Korps* to form two regiment-strong *Kampfgruppen* and supply the LXXXVII. *Armee-Korps*. The *Wehrmachtbericht* reported on the fights on 25 October 1944:

"Concentrated attacks from the south and east against the region of Tilburg – Hertogenbosch were brought to a standstill under the firing of numerous enemy tanks. In Hertogenbosch bitter street fighting has erupted."

As a result, *SS-Obergruppenführer* and *General der Waffen-SS* Bittrich ordered the 363. *Infanterie-Division* as well as the 10. *SS-Panzer-Division* "Frundsberg" under his command to each transfer two *Grenadier-Bataillone* to the Maas through Veenendaal – Culemborg.

Under the command of *SS-Obersturmbannführer* Traupe (*Kdr.* of the *SS-Panzer-Grenadier-Regiment* 22), both battalions moved into a bridgehead position over the Maas at Heusden on 27 October 1944. On 29/30 October 1944, when British troops were able to break through to Waalwijk, a battalion of the *SS-Kampfgruppe* "Traupe" received the order to march into this region. Deployed to both of the most important bridgeheads over the Maas, the men of the SS-*Kampfgruppe* "Traupe" ensured the mostly orderly retreat of the 15. *Armee* behind the Maas.

On 8/9 November 1944 the bridgeheads were given up, the bridges detonated, and a uniform main front taken along the Maas. The *SS-Kampfgruppe* "Traupe" marched back to the Arnhem region and was back under the command of SS-*Brigadeführer* and *Generalmajor der Waffen*-SS Harmel.

Conflicts in the Linnich Region

The section "Fremde Heere West" of the OKH wrote a study on 15 November 1944 on the adversarial offenses on the western front. It indicated that the focus was on the mid-Maas, at Metz, as well as at Aachen. The American 9th Army (seven infantry divisions and three tank divisions with a total of approximately 1,200 tanks) was located in the Aachen region, and could advance to Cologne in a wide front. Hitler made comments with regard to the forthcoming attack from the region north of Aachen with multiple orders that partially read like phrases:

"1. Protection of your own troop, heaviest losses for the enemy,
2. strong organization of the artillery,
3. preparation for extensive destruction, mining and tank traps,
4. selection of the command posts so that the command will not be cut off during tank
*   breakthroughs,*
5. forceful reconnaissance to maintain a clear picture of the enemy,
6. arrangements so that no Maas bridges fall into the hands of the
*   opponent undestroyed,*
7. reinforcement of the Siegfried Line up to the last sector,
8. Dispersal of the 15. Armee *for the purpose of training of reserves, in addition the*
*   release of the 10.* SS-Panzer Division *and the 363.* Volksgrenadier-Division."

Already one day after the study of the OKW on 16 November 1944 the American major offensive began! On the first day the U.S. troops, at roughly 4 km wide, were able to break through the German main front at Immendorf. On 18 November 1944, when American troops occupied Geilenkirchen, the relief of the 10. *SS-Panzer-Division* "Frundsberg" was already underway by the 6. *Fallschirmjäger-Division* (*Generalmajor* Erdmann).

If the German units had put up heavy resistance in some places against the American troops since the landing in Normandy, the losses of the U.S. troops in this offensive would have reached especially high numbers. Until 21 November 1944 (the day the encircled Aachen surrendered) the OKH assumed that the opponent had lost roughly 20,000 men in the past five days (sic!)!

Though the German troops were regarded as having a high morale, primarily the great lack of fuel and air support again became noticeable. On 21 November 1944 the *Oberbefehlshaber* "West" reported:

"the defensive battle at Aachen significantly debilitated the Heeresgruppe *'B.' The 47. and 340.* Volksgrenadier-Division, *and possibly also the 352.* Volksgrenadier-Division *were pulled into the battle and the 12.* Volks-Grenadier-Division *could not be liberated. The 9.*

and 116. Panzer-Division, *as well as the 3. and 15*. Panzer-Grenadier-Division *were bound for the duration of the battle; the 10*. SS-Panzer-Division *must also likely be deployed."*

As *OKH-Reserve*, the 10. *SS-Panzer-Division* "Frundsberg" reached the 5. *Panzer-Armee* (*General* von Manteuffel) in the Erkelenz region through Emmerich – Wesel – Krefeld – Mönchen-Gladbach. Shoved to the left flank of the XXXXVII. *Panzer-Korps* (*General der Panzertruppen* Freiherr von Lüttwitz) west of Linnich, at the front between the 340. *Volks-Grenadier-Division* (right flank of the LXXXI. *Armee-Korps*) and the severely debilitated 9. *Panzer-Division*, the old main front at Geilenkirchen was to be recaptured and the enemy hit in the flank.

Deployment of the 10. *SS-Panzer-Division* "Frundsberg" at Linnich
(22. November – 6 December 1944)

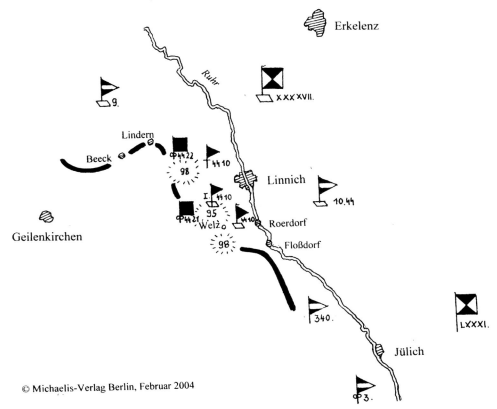

On the evening of 22 November 1944 the I./*SS-Panzer-Grenadier-Regiment* 22 (SS-*Hauptsturmführer* Euling) arrived for the assault on Hill 98 west of Linnich, and the II./ *SS-Panzer-Grenadier-Regiment* 21 (SS-*Hauptsturmführer* Siebert) on Hill 95. The late-arriving III./*SS-Panzer-Grenadier-Regiment* 21 (SS-*Hauptsturmführer* Richter), as well as the II./*SS-Panzer-Grenadier-Regiment* 22 (SS-*Hauptsturmführer* Schatz), arrived the next morning for action. The battalion of the *SS-Panzer-Grenadier-Regiment* 21 was for the advance on Ederen, while the battalion of the *SS-Panzer-Grenadier-Regiment* 22 was in the battle for Beeck.

For reinforcement of the *Panzer-Grenadiere* the SS-*Panzer-Jäger-Abteilung* 10 was pulled to the region of the *SS-Panzer-Grenadier-Regiment* 22, and the II./*SS-Panzer-Regiment* 10 to the region of the *SS-Panzer-Grenadier-Regiment*. The SS-*Panzer-Aufklärungs-Abteilung* 10 moved into position at Welz.

On 29 November 1944, when the American 84ᵗʰ and 102ⁿᵈ Infantry Divisions were on the offensive, there was further heavy combat with heavy losses on each side. The German artillery was able to take the American provisions and attack operations under fire with an exceptional supply of ammunition with a devastating effect! Enemy invasions in the region of the 10. *SS-Panzer-Division* "Frundsberg" were settled mostly in a counterthrust.

As the situation with the 340. *Volks-Grenadier-Division* in the Floßdorf region became critical, *SS-Brigadeführer* and *Generalmajor der Waffen-SS* Harmel formed a supporting *Kampfgruppe* from sections of the:

- *SS-Panzer-Aufklärungs-Abteilung* 10
- *SS-Panzer-Jäger-Abteilung* 10
- *SS-Panzer-Pionier-Bataillon* 10

They marched into the Floßdorf region, which was taken shortly afterwards into the area of responsibility of the 10. *SS-Panzer-Division*.

On 1 December 1944 the U.S. troops were again able to break through the main front and reach Linnich. After intense street fighting the city fell on 2/3 December 1944 into the hands of the Americans. However, without having formed a bridgehead over the Ruhr, the attack was initially abandoned. The 10. *SS-Panzer-Division* "Frundsberg," severely battered in the heavy combat, was able to retreat behind the Ruhr and move into prepared defensive positions. A few days later a transfer order from Hitler followed for the 10. *SS-Panzer-Division* "Frundsberg." The division was to stand by as reserves of the 6. *Panzer-Armee* for the Ardennes Offensive.

A former member of the *SS-Panzer-Aufklärungs-Abteilung* 10 recalls the fighting in the Linnich region:

"We were deployed at the Arnhem bridgehead until 18 November 1944, until we were relieved by Fallschirmeinheiten. *Only a few days of rest and replenishment, then we were loaded in Boetichen and supplied to a new area of action. The journey was short, as in Reydt (Rhineland) we unloaded again. We went in a motorized march into the Aachen combat area. The* Aufklärungs-Abteilung *was assigned to the Wels-Rurdorf sector.*

On an early afternoon a young Ordonnanzoffizier *arrived with the order of the* Abteilung *to reestablish contact with the* SS-Panzer-Grenadier-Regiment 22.

There was excessive heavy artillery fire over the entire combat sector, and enemy fighter-bombers swept over the positions and turned each movement into an impossibility.

Because the situation was completely unexplained, we advanced northwest after a few hundred meters and caught sight of entrenched soldiers. We thought we had completed our assignment, but upon coming closer we realized with horror that the Americans were located in front of us. The low December sun had blinded us so much that we didn't recognize the Americans until later. Just 50 meters separated us from the opponent. If the American thought we were deserters there was one thing they hadn't reckoned with; our reaction time was short, and we quickly took flight. The surprise was great for us, as we had not yet expected the opponent. Things had to be handled in order to prevent a continued advance. The situation was reported to the section and reinforcement requested. Not long, and a Heereskompanie *arrived. They also immediately attacked, but advanced only a few meters and remained under losses. The* Kompanieführer, *a* Leutnant, *now panic-stricken, wanted to retreat again, which we emphatically prevented. Fortunately the* Strafvollstreckungszug *of our division came and was deployed to the right of us. Contact with* Regiment 22 *still did not exist. Unfortunately, in the course of the night the* Heereskompanie *withdrew, for which sections of our* SS-Pionier-Bataillon 10 *came to the main front.*

With the increasing light of day the enemy artillery fire intensified, suggesting further enemy attacks. Until midday nothing took place. But then hell broke loose. Fighter-bombers attacked our positions, let alone tremendous artillery fire. Then smoke was fired—a sign that the opponent was attacking. Everyone was ready for defense and tried to see through the smoke. Then infantry fire began and finally the smoke dissipated. The Americans had broken through between us and Regiment 22 – the Strafvollstreckungszug *had already retreated! From the left flank came the bad news that contact no longer existed with our own section to the left. Flares that shot up from the edge of the town Rurdorf made our position visible. It was clear that we had to hold the position until dark in order to connect with our own troop. Artillery fire was ordered to impede the advancement of the opponent.*

The fighter bombers even helped us – they did not recognize the lines and dropped bombs on their own troops. It was certainly also regrettable for the Americans, but for us the help came at the right time. Then a new shock – the Americans were situated with tanks on the Linnich – Rurdorf street in front of the town, directly at our backs. We also received fire from there. In the darkness we succeeded in retreating from the enemy unhindered. We immediately moved into a new position in the complete defense of Rurdorf. Late in the evening a small Stoßtrupp *was put together to get out a wounded* Rottenführer *of our* Zug *who was in the hospital. The hospital was halfway to Linnich and was occupied by the Americans. The* Rottenführer *was able to be brought out, and thus avoided captivity. Sturmmann Thomalla met a special fate. The poor guy had a high fever the entire day but couldn't go back. Where the evacuation was supposed to take place, he fell due to artillery fire. In Arnhem, during the destruction of bunkers Thomalla had distinguished himself in front of the* Abteilungskommandeur *and received the Iron Cross.*

There was artillery fire on our position the entire night that intensified until the morning. Suddenly there was great yelling and shooting, as the Americans had broken into Rurdorf. The sections of the SS-Pionier-Bataillon *10 that were to the left of us had already evaded and left their positions. We also didn't stay long. The Americans had come into Rurdorf, and we were once again cut off. We had to get over the Rur as safely as possible.*

It all worked out relatively well. A footbridge over the Rur was held by the Strafvollstrekkungszug. *At dawn we headed to the other side of the shore to prepared front lines. The footbridge was detonated. But there was a rude awakening. The front lines were to have been occupied – but nothing of the sort was to be seen. Thus, we had to occupy the positions – again, contact to the left or to the right did not exist. What was going on? The Americans were shooting again with artillery. They believed they would be able to smoke us out with phosphorus grenades. With damp cloths on our mouths and noses the men stood in the water. The fighter-bombers provided the background music. In the course of the day contact was able to be made with the unit that actually belonged to this sector. Around evening a* Zugführer *with a reporter searched for the command post of the army in order to clarify the situation. After initial discrepancies and unwillingness to understand, the matter was quickly settled.*

The SS-Panzer-Aufklärungs-Abteilung *10 gathered in Hottorf. They were relieved as fast as possible and led back to Hottorf. Halfway there two* Schützenpanzerwagen *approached to pick up the correct men to be taken along. While the entire section from the commander to the last man had swam across the Rur, that – by the footbridge – remains spared!"*

Replenishment in the Cologne Region

After just a two week assignment in the Linnich region the 10. *SS-Panzer-Division* "Frundsberg" was already detached from the main front at the beginning of December 1944 in order to stand by for the Ardennes Offensive. The war diary of the OKW remarked regarding this:

"On 6 December 1944 the Führer *once again pointed out the significance it holds to pull out the 10.* SS-Panzer-Division *during the current decline of fighting and to replace them with the 340.* Infanterie-Division."

As a result, on 6 December 1944 the relief of the 10. SS-*Panzer-Division* "Frundsberg" by the 340. *Volks-Grenadier-Division* and assembly in the Erkelenz region began. From there the *SS* unit, weakened by the previous approximately ten-day heavy combat, transferred to the Blatzheim – Kerpen – Euskirchen region to be replenished there as reserves of the 6. *Panzer-Armee* for the Ardennes Offensive. Four days later the *SS* unit reported the numbers of the heavy weapons at the OB "West":

	Required	Actual	in Demand	Deficit	Excess
Panzer V "Panther"	60	4	25	31	
Panzer IV (7.5 cm)	30	10	34		14
Sturmgeschütze	21	11	3	7	
Heavy Pak	28	6	15	7	
Light *Feldhaubitzen*	37	37			
Heavy *Feldhaubitzen*	18	18			
10 cm *Kanonen*	4	8			4

Comparison with the requirements of a *Heeresdivision* shows similar numbers. The presumption that the *Waffen-SS* was fundamentally preferred and more heavily equipped was disproved. On the contrary, the 10. *SS-Panzer-Division* "Frundsberg" had only one instead of two *Panzer-Abteilungen* for roughly two years, and thereby moreso resembled a *Panzer-Grenadier-Division*!

Although the 6. *Panzer-Armee* was supplied for the Ardennes Offensive beginning on 16 December 1944, the 10. *SS-Panzer-Division* "Frundsberg" was not deployed, and was also not in the heavy but unsuccessful fighting of the annihilation of the American 101st Airborne Division encircled in Bastogne. Both heavy, combat supporting units that practically had the required equipment at their command—the *SS-Panzer-Artillerie-Regiment* 10 as well as the *SS-Panzer-Flak-Abteilung* 10—provided sections of the 6. *Panzer-Armee*. Under the command of the 9. *SS-Panzer-Division* "Hohenstaufen," the III./ *SS-Panzer-Artillerie-Regiment* 10, among others, took part in the capture of St. Viths.

During the four weeks of rest and replenishment the division finally received after roughly 24 months the I. (Panther)/*SS-Panzer-Regiment* 10 from Grafenwöhr. It initially had only half of the required strength (the other half went to the 9. *SS-Panzer-Division* "Hohenstaufen"), however, it brought a great reinforcement of the division with 25 new Panzer V "Panthers." The KTB/OKW declared the 10. *SS-Panzer-Division* now "completely fit for war."

During the resting phase a "memory book" was prepared for the members of the division. *SS-Brigadeführer* and *Generalmajor der Waffen-SS* Harmel wrote the foreword:

"Frundsberger!

Two years have passed since the formation of the 10. SS-Panzer-Division 'Frundsberg.' The first year of combat is behind you.

Bravely and fearlessly you have fought, no matter when, where, and against whom.

With courage you have survived the baptism of fire, and have more than once proven that you are fully prepared even under the most difficult of conditions

By your courage, exemplary bravery, your relentlessness, your incredible energy in attack, and your grim determination in defense you have all, without exception, each contributing at and with his weapon, that this "young division" has within a short time become a Kampfverband *feared at all times by the enemy.*

All units of this division are equally included.

Frundsberger! With this, you place yourselves as equals on the side of the older divisions of the Waffen-SS *in inseparable loyalty and comradeship to these.*

I am convinced that in this new year of combat, which will not be easier, you will persist in exactly the same fashion as in the past.

Buczaz – Caen – St. Lamteot – Arnhem – Nijmwegen and Zinnoda! They are the great days of the demonstration of your worth, milestones on the warpath of the Frundsberger in the year 1944!

This book is dedicated to you as a memorial of your deeds.

You should proudly take it in your hands later, show your boys and girls, and be able to say: I also took part in this!

Again, to the enemy!

Always remain young, bright lads, incredibly courageous and brave, and always so alert as once in the battles of the year 1944!

Always remain good and modest SS *men as before who stand by the proven battle cry of the Frundsberger:*

Dran, drauf und durch!

Long live the Führer.*"*

Repair of a Panzer III with KWK 7.5 cm long.

Zugmaschine (18 ton) and *Tieflader.*

Mission in Alsace

After the American troops withdrew from Alsace through the German Ardennes Offensive and were transferred to the north, Hitler planned another offensive—not least for the relief of the units in the Ardennes. Through attacks of the 1. *Armee* from the region on both sides of Bitsch toward the south into the Vosges and the 19. *Armee* from the Straßburg region northwest through the enemy Rhine front toward Hagenau – Brumath, the U.S. troops already at Weißenburg were to be cut off from lines of communication and annihilated.

The offensiv—as of 25 December 1944 referred to as Operation "Nordwind"—began on the night of 31 December 1944. After the XIII. SS-*Armee-Korps* (*SS-Gruppenführer* and *Generalleutnant der Waffen-SS* Simon[32]), attacking within the framework of the 1. *Armee* and the LXXXIX. *Armee-Korps*, could only achieve meager territorial gain, the operation was soon aborted on 3 January 1945.

In the night of 5 January 1945 the 19. *Armee* (*Oberbefehlshaber* "Oberrhein" – *Reichsführer-SS* Himmler)—which up to this point had not yet reported—was to advance northwest with all available forces in order to make contact with the troops of the 1. *Armee* who were pushed into defense.

After the American resistance could hardly be broken, and their own infantry forces became increasingly weaker, on 7 January 1945 Hitler authorized the deployment of further units to the *Heeresgruppe* "G." As a result, the following received their assignment and transfer orders:

- 10. *SS-Panzer-Division* "Frundsberg
- 7. *Fallschirmjäger-Division*
- 47. *Volks-Grenadier-Division*
- 11. *Panzer-Division*
- 2. *Gebirgs-Division*

Two days later Hitler once again pointed out to the *Oberbefehlshaber* "West" and "Oberrhein" the significance of the successful conclusion of the battle for Hagenau and the annihilation of the enemy forces between the lower Vosges and the Rhine. On 11 January 1945 he ordered:

"The attack of the XXXIX. Panzer-Korps *at Rittershofen has fallen through and the enemy has shifted his focus there. Therefore, the 7.* Fallschirmjäger-Division, *reinforced by the* Sturm-Geschütz-Brigaden *667 and 384, and the 10.* SS-Panzer-Division *from the*

---

32 See Appendix 7

Forstfeld – Beinheim region will be positioned for attack as soon as possible through Röschwoog toward Drusenheim to make contact with the 503. Infanterie-Division. *The objective of the attack is (bypassing the Haguenau Forest to the south) to break through to the west through Bischweiler, and in conjunction with the attack of the 1.* Armee *(6. SS-Gebirgs-Division and 256.* Infanterie-Division*) to destroy the opponent north of the Haguenau Forest toward Zinsweiler and Niederbronn."*

On 12 January 1945 the region Forstfeld – Beinheim was placed under the command of the XXXIX. *Panzer-Korps (General der Panzertruppen* Decker[33]*).* The XXXIX. *Panzer-Korps* in turn came under the command of the *Oberbefehlshaber* "Oberrhein." The 10. *SS-Panzer-Division* "Frundsberg" began the loading of the train in the present quarters of Erftstadt – Euskirchen – Bonn, and as of 14/15 January 1945 reached the region west of Bühl. The crossing began immediately on the left side of the Rhine shore in the bridgehead position of Gambsheim.

On 17 January 1945 SS-*Brigadeführer* and *Generalmajor* Harmel deployed the *SS-Panzer-Regiment* 10 to expand the relatively small bridgehead as a line of departure for the upcoming attack. Concerning this, the KTB/OKW note

"The 10. SS-Panzer-Division *advanced to the west from the bridgehead."*

Two days later the unsuccessful attack began toward Brumath, during which the units withdrew to the lines of departure due to the heavy losses from the enemy air force and artillery during the evening.

General der Panzertruppen Decker decided to transfer the focus of the attack to the north toward the Haguenau Forest. For the 10. *SS-Panzer-Division* "Frundsberg" this meant a regrouping. The neighboring 553. *Volks-Grenadier-Division* took over the region of the *SS-Panzer-Grenadier-Regiment* 21, which until now was situated on the left border of the division, and which now transferred to the right border of the division.

On 24 January 1945 the *SS-Panzer-Grenadier-Regiment* 22 mustered at Oberhofen together with the I./*SS-Panzer-Regiment* 10 from the Rohrweiler region, and the *SS-Panzer-Grenadier-Regiment* 21 together with the II./*SS-Panzer-Regiment* 10 from the Schirrheim region toward Hagenau. Both attacks remained under heavy American resistance fire similar to the entire front of Operation "Nordwind" before reaching their target. As a result the offensive was abandoned.

33 See Appendix 7

For half a year the 10. *SS-Panzer-Division* "Frundsberg" was frequently pulled from action after cessation of fighting and transferred for participation in a new offensive—this time in the east again. On 3 February 1945 the relief began by sections of the 553. *Volks-Grenadier-Division* in the south, and by sections of the 21. *Panzer-Division* in the north.

Deployment of the 10. SS-*Panzer-Division* "Frundsberg"
14 January – 3 February 1945

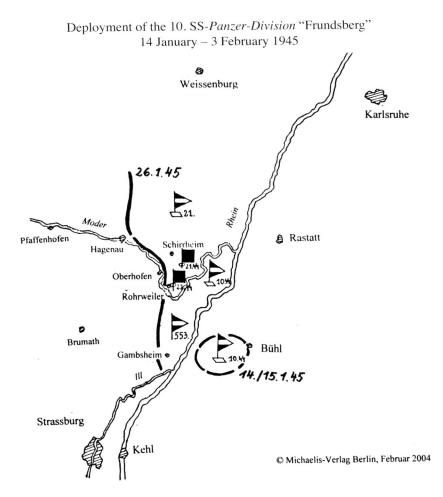

© Michaelis-Verlag Berlin, Februar 2004

Mission in Pomerania

On 12 January 1945 the Soviet Winter Offensive had begun. In three days the Red army advanced from multiple bridgeheads on both sides of Warsaw at a 400 km width towards the west. Oberschlesien was overrun and East Prussia threatened with being cut off. The German military's demand to bring up troops of the 6. (*SS-*) *Panzer-Armee* from the west, as well as the *Heeresgruppe* "Kurland," situated at positions that were lost, to Pomerania was rejected by Hitler.

For this, as of 21 January 1945 the *Heeresgruppe* "Weichsel" was formed hastily. *Reichsführer-SS* Himmler, who was appointed *Oberbefehlshaber* of the new *Heeresgruppe* on 25 January 1945, arrived with his *Befehlszug* "Steiermark" in Deutsch-Krone, and was to close the torn front between Glogau and Elbing. A gap of 150 km existed here between the 9. *Armee* and the *Heeresgruppe* "Weichsel!"

The 1st Belarusian Front under Marshal Zhukov succeeded in advancing on Berlin along the Netze and Warthe, and formed significant bridgeheads over the Oder between Frankfurt and Küstrin. On 30 January 1945 the Soviets ceased further attacks, although the possibility would have existed to immediately advance on Berlin. Supply difficulties and lack of discipline of the Red Army soldiers were the reasons for this. The line Konitz – Ratzebuhr – Deutsch Krone – Pyritz to the Oder across from Schwedt constituted the front in Pomerania at the beginning of February 1945.

The 2nd Belarusian Front under Marshal Rokossowskij had the task of occupying Pomerania and averting the danger of a German attack at the right flank of the 1st Belarusian Front. The head of the *Generalstab des Heeres*, *Generaloberst* Guderian, with the supply of the 6. (*SS-*) *Panzer-Armee* from the west had already suggested such an offensive.[34] Hitler rejected the supply of this *Panzer-Armee*, however, with the reasoning that the relief of Budapest was of higher priority. Thus, in the next days an alternative plan was developed.

As of 26 January 1945 the new formation of the 11. *Armee* from the staff of the *Oberkommando* "Oberrhein" as well as *Ersatz-* and *Ausbildungseinheiten* began. In addition, various active troops received the order to march. On 31 January 1945 the KTB/OKW noted:

---

34 Guderian planned to advance on the flank of the Soviet troops on the Oder with two *Panzer-Korps* from the region southeast of Stettin (today Szczecin in Poland). By doing so, this was to give their own forces west of the Oder time to prepare for the upcoming assault. Furthermore, the German units along the Baltic Sea to Danzig (today Gdansk in Poland) were able to organize and initiate a planned retreat. From the Guben – Glogau (today Glogów in Poland) region German troops were likewise to form northeast and make contact with the *Nordgruppe*.

"Order to examine the question, under what premises the 10. SS-Panzer-Division can be released to the east. Regardless, the division is to withdraw, whereby the Führer *proceeds on the assumption that a major offensive at Orscholz-Riegel or on the Saar front is initially not to be expected."*

A few days later the order followed for the transfer to Pomerania. Within the framework of the XXXIX. *Panzer-Korps* the 10. SS-*Panzer-Division* "Frundsberg" (strength: approximately 10,000 men) reached Stettin as of 5 February 1945 via railway. As of 10 February 1945 sections arrived through Nuremberg – Saalfeld – Halle – Berlin with the following organization:

- *Divisionsstab* with *Begleit- und Feldgendarmerie-Kompanie*
- *SS-Panzer-Grenadier-Regiment* 21 with three battalions
- *SS-Panzer-Grenadier-Regiment* 22 with three battalions
- *SS-Panzer-Artillerie-Regiment* 10 with I.-III. *Abteilung* (with three batteries and four *Geschütze* 10.5 cm *Feldhaubitzen*) and IV. *Abteilung* (10 cm *Kanonen*)
- *SS-Panzer-Pionier-Bataillon* 10
- *SS-Panzer-Jäger-Abteilung* 10 with three companies
- *SS-Panzer-Aufklärungs-Abteilung* 10 with five companies
- *SS-Panzer-Nachrichten-Abteilung* 10 with two companies
- *SS-Panzer-Flak-Abteilung* 10 with three companies
- *SS-Panzer-Regiment* 10 with I. (Panther) and II. (Panzer IV) *Abteilung*

A former member of the *SS-Panzer-Grenadier-Regiment* 22 recalls:

"On 2 February 1945 the opponent attacked us the entire day with artillery. Around evening it was calmer. My comrade Jenkel and I leaned under the open house door of our quarters and talked. He spoke of his home, of their large yard in Pomerania, and of his sister, to whom he was quite attached.

No one could guess in this moment that already the next day our division would be released from the front in Alsace to be thrown into Pomerania on the eastern front. An artillery assault interrupted us. We pulled back further into the house entrance – a piercing scream and Jenkel plunged into the cellar. There he collapsed dead – a piece of shrapnel hit him in the cardiac region. Away with the dream of the yard in Pomerania. In 1979 I found his grave at the military cemetery in Brühl!

As of 3 February 1945 our 13. (Infanteriegeschütz) Kompanie drove in a motorized march left of the Rhine to Landau/Pfalz and loaded there toward Stettin. We had just finished with the loading when the sirens howled. Air raid alarm. Most went into the assigned shelters. But we – six men – we 'old Landser*' naturally saw it as beneath us, and remained at our card game. We hardly said ''false alarm,' when the fighter-bombers already dropped their bombs and with aircraft weapons attacked the railway grounds.*

We were able to suddenly dash from the wagons. The wagons were pushed back and forth from the explosions. There was considerable damage done to the tracks and numerous trains. By some miracle nothing happened to our transport train or us 'old Landser.' Through Heilbronn – Crailsheim – Nuremberg we continued toward Pomerania."

A former member of the *SS-Panzer-Pionier-Bataillon* 10 recalls the transport to Stettin:

"On 7 February 1945 we set out with a large ferry on the right shore of the Rhine and were unloaded. We continued across through Germany. The damage from the bombs on the train tracks forced the transport trains to constantly change direction. Where is it going? The rumor, to Lake Balaton, persisted. During a stop in Halle I heard shouts: Sturmmann Friedrich! My comrade Friedrich greeted his parents. They had heard the Soldatensender West – English – *who announced that the 10.* SS-Panzer-Division *'Frundsberg' was being transferred to the east. The* Pionier-*Bataillon comes through Halle around this time and is expected in Stettin. The English knew better than our* Führer. *We unloaded in Stettin. The train station was full of freight trains. The wagons were mostly open, and we served ourselves cheese, rolls as big as a car wheel. Only bread wasn't available, but a tremendous lot of jam."*

On 15 February 1945 the unit marched from Stettin within the framework of the XXXIX. *Panzer-Korps* (*General der Panzertruppen* Decker) through Altdamm (today Dąbie in Poland) to Stargard. Already the next day the German Operation "Sonnenwende" began. The 11. *Armee*[35] (roughly 80,000 men), under the command of *SS-Obergruppenführer* and *General der Waffen-SS* Steiner, formed up from the line Madü-See along the Ihne – Reetz (today Recz in Poland) – Kallies for attack on the Berlinchen (today Barlinek in Poland) – Friedeberg (today Strzelce Krajeńskie in Poland) region:

- *Korps* "H'rnlein" with the 9. *Fallschirmjäger-Division* between the Oder and Madü-See
- XXXIX. *Panzer-Korps* with *Panzer-Division* "Holstein," 10. *SS-Panzer-Division* "Frundsberg," 4. *SS-Polizei-Panzer-Grenadier-Division* and *Kampfgruppe*/28. *SS-Freiwilligen-Grenadier-Division* "Wallonien" between Madü-See and Faule Ihna
- III. (Germanic) *SS-Panzer-Korps* with 11. *SS-Freiwilligen-Panzer-Grenadier-Division* "Nordland," *Kampfgruppe*/27. *SS-Freiwilligen-Grenadier-Division* "Langemarck," 23. *SS-Freiwilligen-Panzer-Grenadier-Division* "Nederland," as well as the 281. *Infanterie-Division* between Ihna and Reetz
- *Panzer-Korps* "Munzel" with *Führer-Begleit- und Führer-Grenadier-Division* for securing the flank at Neu-Wedell (today Drawno in Poland) and the Drawa

---

35 Initially the 11. *Armee* had taken over command of the line from the mouth of the Finow Canal into the Oder to the Jastrow – Ratzebuhr – Neustettin (today Szczecinek in Poland) line. The headquarters were first located at Crössinsee and then transferred to Plathe.

- X. *SS-Armee-Korps* with SS-*Kampfgruppe* "Schulz-Streeck," 402. Division z. b. V. and 5. *Jäger-Division* for a binding attack toward Kallies
- Korps "von Tettau" z. b. V. with *Einsatz-Divisionen* "Bärwalde" and "Köslin," as well as the 163. *Infanterie-Division* as left army flank.

The XXXIX. *Panzer-Korps* was to initially reach the Schönings-Kanal and join from the left to the right with sections of the 4. SS-*Panzer-Grenadier-Division*, the *Kampfgruppe/28*. SS-*Freiwilligen-Grenadier-Division* "Wallonien," and the 10. SS-*Panzer-Division* "Frundsberg," as well as the *Panzer-Division* "Holestein."

The order for the 10. *SS-Panzer-Division* "Frundsberg" stated to attack on the morning of 16 February 1945 from the region of Schlötenitz toward Margaretenhof – Uslar. In addition to the fact that the *SS-Panzer-Grenadier-Regiment* 22 and the I. (Panther)/*SS-Panzer-Regiment* 10 were still in transport, it was made difficult for the division's command that they did not previously have any opportunities to familiarize themselves with the area! The attack remained exactly like that of the *Panzer-Division* "Holstein" in the Damnitz – Warnitz region. The *Wehrmachtbericht* reported for this day:

"In the southern part of Pomerania between the Oder and Reets heavy attacks and resistance combat had broken out."

After the 2. *SS-Panzer-Grenadier-Division* to the southeast had succeeded in breaking into enemy positions at Blumberg and Brallenthin, the *General der Panzertruppen* Decker shifted the focus of attack there and ordered the transfer of the 10. SS-*Panzer-Division* "Frundsberg" to this region.

On the night of 16 February 1945 the entire division—including the missing sections arriving in the meantime from transport—assembled in the region of the 2. *SS-Panzer-Grenadier-Division* at the Ihna bridgehead Blumenberg. The 10. *SS-Panzer-Division* was to advance from here through Muscherin – Lübtow and fight free the encircled troops from Pyritz.

On the afternoon of 17 February 1945 the *SS-Panzer-Aufklärungs-Abteilung* 10 mustered with the II. /*SS-Panzer-Regiment* 10 and the *SS-Panzer-Grenadier-Regiment* 22 for attack. Schöningsthal and Sallentin were able to be taken. The I. /*SS-Panzer-Regiment* 10 was placed under the command of their left neighbor (the 4. *SS-Panzer-Grenadier-Division*) in the fight for Dölitz. The right neighbor was the *Kampfgruppe/28*. SS-*Freiwilligen-Grenadier-Division* "Wallonien," which was able to reach the Lindenberge.

While troops of the adjoining III. (Germanic) *SS-Panzer-Korps* reached Arnwalde after intense fighting and began the evacuation of approximately 5,000 civilians and wounded, the new advance of the XXXIX. *Panzer-Korps* was left undone. On 18 February 1945 the main front of the corps ran from the southern edge of the Madü-See over the Lindenberge – Sallenthin – Muscherin toward east of Dölitz.

The unanticipated Soviet resistance, as well as the realization of the supply of strong new enemy tank units, caused the *Heeresgruppe* "Weichsel" to cease Operation "Sonnenwende" after only three days "*...in order to avoid the worthless wearing out of the* Angriffsverbände."

The *Lagebuch* of the *Heeresgruppe* "Weichsel" notes on 20 February 1945:

"With the attack from the north, preparations of the 2ⁿᵈ and 1ˢᵗ (Soviet) Guards Tank Army have not been disrupted due to the new forces the enemy has supplied for attack."

For the 10. *SS-Panzer-Division* "Frundsberg" this meant the withdrawal of the troops behind the Faule Ihna. During the retreat there was an attack of the Red Army that led to heavy close combat in Muscherin on 19 February 1945. Because the 4. *SS-Panzer-Grenadier-Division* was transferred to West Prussia, the 10. *SS-Panzer-Division* (division command point at Schöneberg) took over their positions in the course of withdrawal and reduction of the front. The main front ran roughly 5 km south of Stargard.

On 23 February 1945 the XXXIX. *Panzer-Korps* was pulled from the front and transferred to middle Germany. Two days later, from the Stargard assembly area the transport of the 10. *SS-Panzer-Division* "Frundsberg" to the region of Fürstenwalde/Oder at the disposal of the 9. *Armee* began. Here the Soviet bridgehead was to be crushed.

While the transports to the 9. *Armee* were underway, on 1 March 1945 the anticipated Soviet major offensive in Pomerania began along the Ihna. The Red Army was able to cause nearly the entire German front to collapse within a few hours. The Soviet units were able to disrupt contact between the Panzer-AOK 3[36] and the 2. *Armee*. At Reetz, the opposing units advanced between the X. *SS-Armee-Korps* and the III. (Germanic) *SS-Panzer-Korps* through the main front, and finally encircled the former corps at Dramburg (today Drawsko Pomorskie in Poland). Only sections were able to escape the annihilation around 5 March 1945.

---

36 After the AOK 11 was transferred west in March 1945, the *Panzer-AOK* 3 took over the entire command at the forefront of Stargard.

The III. (Germanic) SS-*Panzer-Korps* was forced toward the Baltic Sea by the swift enemy thrust, its left flank constantly folding toward the north in order to prevent an encirclement. On 2 March 1945 the main front already ran on the line Madü-See – Freienwalde. The transports of the 10. *SS-Panzer-Division* "Frundsberg" to the 9. *Armee* were stopped and ordered back to the Köslin (today Koszalin in Poland) region. From here, Hitler planned to re-establish contact with the 2. *Armee* with an attack to the east. At the same time the Soviet units advancing toward the Baltic Sea were to be separated from the lines of communication and annihilated. Utopia!

The Battles in Pomerania
(16 February-20 March 1945)

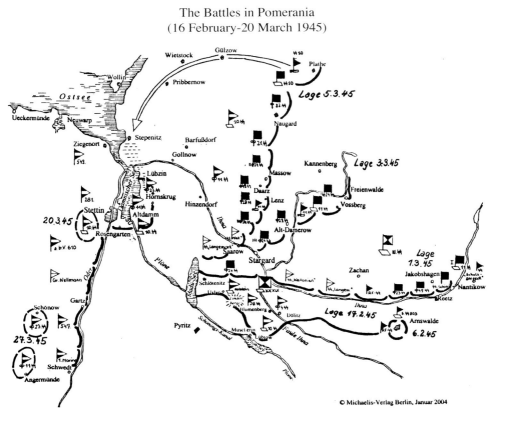

While both cornerstones of Freienwalde and Stargard were able to be maintained—the latter by Walloon *SS-Freiwilligen*—the front in between collapsed. The III. (Germanic) *SS-Panzer-Korps* ordered to retreat to the line Massow – Stargard.

The *Oberbefehlshaber* of the 3. *Panzer-Armee*, *Generaloberst* Raus,[37] realized that Hitler's order to attack could not be executed, and ordered *SS-Brigadeführer* and *Generalmajor der Waffen-SS* Harmel to secure the Regnitz region and take in the remainder of the units that were battered further east (X. *SS-Armee-Korps* and *Korpsgruppe* "Tettau"). However, this could also not be realized.

On 2/3 March 1945 *SS-Brigadeführer* Harmel ordered sections of the *SS-Panzer-Grenadier-Regiment* 22 together with sections of the *SS-Panzer-Aufklärungs-Abteilung* 10 to the region of Plathe – Naugard (today Nowogard in Poland). On 4 March 1945 sections of the *SS-Panzer-Regiment* 10 followed, and thus hindered the quick capture of the towns by the Red Army. A former member of the 20. *Waffen-Grenadier-Division* of the SS (Estonian No. 1) came to the III./*SS-Panzer-Grenadier-Regiment* 21, and recalls the heavy fighting for Naugard:

"In Pillau [today the Russian city of Baltiysk] *we last 8 men of the* SS-Flak-Abteilung *20 were shipped to Stettin on January 1945 and transferred there to the Stargard region. The population was very happy to see us because they believed that we would stop the Russians. We were accommodated with single families and treated like their own children. My vehicle had transmission damage, and I was hauled to Naugard, where an army repair shop was to perform the work. Replacements parts were in short supply, and I had to remain in Naugard and wait for the missing parts – I had a nice spring!*

At this time I was the only SS *man in the city. In the schnapps factory there was a* Pionier-Einheit *of the army, whose cook took care of me. One morning the* Instandsetzungsgruppe *(it all consisted of men between 50 and 60 years old) had withdrawn. After one hour the factory was cleared out. The* Heerespioniere *had already marched off the evening before. Also, the owner of the factory left the city before midnight with her 10-year-old son with a DKW (Band-aid Bomber) because she feared that the Russians were coming.*

Out on a limb I looked around the house and found 30 liters of gasoline (!), a compass, and a telescopic sight for the hunting rifle, as well as a pistol. I immediately picked up the things. Around 13:00 hours I left the factory toward Gut Willhelmsfeld, which was located one kilometer in front of Naugard. During my forays I came to know a girl who was there as a refugee from East Prussia. I wanted to inform her that a train was standing by to evacuate the civilians. As I turned from the road to the estate, suddenly Russian tanks

---

37 See Appendix 7

Pomerania 1945 – a damaged *Sturmgeschütz* is being hauled off.

appeared and shot with machine guns from the direction of Dabern. Screaming loudly, I ran to the Hof *to alarm everyone. Together we ran over the field to the train station. The train, consisting of freight wagons, was already overcrowded. But I didn't go with them; rather, I went back to the factory. Then I got scared. Was I now the only soldier in Naugard? For hours I hadn't seen a living soul and went back to the city.*

At the market square I met comrades of the 10. SS-Panzer-Division 'Frundsberg.' They showed me the command post of the III./SS-Panzer-Grenadier Regiment 21, in which a dentist practice was accommodated in the second floor. My report that I was shot at by Russian tanks at Gut Wilhelmsfeld was taken with skepticism – no one believed me.

The Führer *at the command post discussed if someone should wake the* Bataillonskommandeur *when suddenly there was a frightful noise and fragments flew in the room. A tank shell had shot out the window. When there was quiet again and the dust had dispersed, it was able to be determined that no one was injured.*

Then a man with suspenders without a uniform jacket stood in the doorway – SS-Sturmbannführer Fritz Richter. For 36 hours he hadn't slept. I made a report, mentioned the 30 liters of gasoline, and received the order to bring everything useful to the command post.

When I returned with my 'precious' freight, I asked to be permitted to stay with the battalion because I had lost my unit. With everything that I had on me (telescopic sight, compass, and pistol) I must have made a good impression with Richter, because he named me his personal reporter by adding: 'if you are farther than three meters from me, without me having ordered you, I will kick you in the ass!'

That was on 3 March 1945.

The next day the Russians attacked, whereby the focus shifted to the train station and to the north of the city. At the railroad embankment and at the train station the Russians had considerable losses, because the company that defended the train station fought bitterly at each platform. In the north the pressure was so strong that heavy street fighting resulted.

When the Russians with tanks were already in the immediate vicinity of the command post, the commander also became a lone fighter. I heard SS-Sturmbannführer *say: 'Everything was much worse before!'*

Five or six tanks were supplied to our battalion – but I had not seen any up to this point. Then the report came: the Zugführer *of the tanks has fallen.*

A comrade put a Russian tank out of action with the Panzerfaust *from the window of an apartment from an upper floor. The city was in flames in all corners, and the companies that fought in the north of Naugard reported again and again handing over houses and streets. There was no longer any reinforcement!*

Suddenly two enemy tanks drove over the market square toward us. One was put out of action with a Panzerfaust, *but the second* Panzerfaust *missed the other. Richter ordered a 'change of position,' during which we were wounded. Over hedges, fences, and gardens we reached a house in which the medical station was set up – my wounded calf had swollen in the meantime and was bleeding heavily.*

Richter handed over command to the Stabsarzt *of the* Luftwaffe *and rode to the division's command post, which was accommodated in an estate. Around approximately 3:00 hours during the night we reached him. Before my* Bataillonskommandeur *was able to make a report,* SS-Brigadeführer *Harmel asked him 'Richter, what are you doing here?'*

Harmel remained ice cold, he didn't approach Richter. He then made a report and said that Naugard could still be held for five to ten hours, and that he had given command over to the Stabsarzt.

What did the Divisionskommandeur *think when he saw the* Bataillonskommandeur *with a dolt like myself? I was in enormous pain. The type of treatment against Richter shocked me! At first it seemed moreso like an arrest than a release into a military hospital.*

Around 5:00 hours we reached Stettin with a vehicle – the military hospital was just closed down – so we came with other wounded by train to the west. Today it is clear to me that I have SS-Sturmbannführer *Richter to thank for coming out of Naugard. It was 42 more years until I saw Richter again!"*

On 5 March 1945 the division's command post was in Rörchen. The I. /SS-Panzer-Artillerie-Regiment 10 was in Glewitz, the II. Abteilung in Marsdorf, the III. Abteilung in Diedrichsdorf, and the IV. Abteilung in Barfußdorf.

During the retreat the SS-Panzer-Aufklärungs-Abteilung 10 lost contact with the SS-Panzer-Grenadier-Regiment 22, and initially moved toward Greifenberg, then towards the southwest to Wietstock. On 6 March 1945 the members of the SS-Panzer-Aufklärungs-Abteilung 10 reached Stepenitz, and on 7/8 March 1945 proceeded with small ships to Ziegendorf over the Stettin lagoon.

The majority of the 10. SS-Panzer-Division retreated to Gollnow (today Goleniów in Poland), and was then situated at the Kicker – Stepenitz River – Neuendorf line. Rechter and the southern neighbor were the remainder of the 23. SS-Freiwilligen-Panzer-Grenadier-Division "Nederland" in the Massow region. After intense combat at Neuendorf (SS-Panzer-Grenadier-Regiment 21) and Gollnow the units retreated during the night of 7 March 1945 into the region around Altdamm, which was intended as a bridgehead.

In addition to the II./*SS-Panzer-Grenadier-Regiment* 21, the II./*SS-Panzer-Grenadier-Regiment* 24 "Danmark," as well as units of the army, were placed under the command of the 23. *SS-Freiwilligen-Panzer-Grenadier-Division* "Nederland," which was maintaining the northern sector of the bridgehead (Lübzin to Hornskrug). Toward the south was the 11. *SS-Freiwilligen-Panzer-Grenadier-Division* "Nordland" with the SS-*Panzer-Aufklärungs-Abteilung* 11 and the *SS-Panzer-Grenadier-Regiment* 23 "Norge" at the line Hornskrug – Autobahn, and the III./*SS-Panzer-Grenadier-Regiment* 24 "Danmark," *SS-Pionier-Bataillon* 11, and *SS-Flak-Abteilung* 11 to Rosengarten. From here the 10. *SS-Panzer-Division* "Frundsberg" was located at the main front. The *SS-Panzer-Flak-Abteilung* 10 and sections of the *SS-Panzer-Aufklärungs-Abteilung* 10 were at Rosengarten and at the Altdamm airport. To the right, at Höckendorf, the XXXII. *Armee-Korps* made contact with the rest of the *Kampfgruppen* of the 27. and 28. *SS-Freiwilligen-Grenadier-Division* "Langemarck" and "Wallonien," as well as the 549. *Volks-Grenadier-Division* and 281. *Infanterie-Division*. The 1. *Marine-Infanterie-Division*, together with the 25. *Panzer-Grenadier-Division* and the *Panzer-Division* "Schlesien," were situated in the south of Greifenhagen to Höckendorf.

Because the German bridgehead could not be annihilated from the movement, the Red Army briefly stopped the attacks and formed for a new attack. On 15 March 1945 the Soviets mustered for the assault on the Altdamm bridgehead after heavy artillery attacks. The *SS-Panzer-Grenadier-Regiment* 22, which was in reserves, was taken from Finkenwalde to the Buchheide Forest. The next day the *Heeresgruppe* "Weichsel" reported:

"1. New military intelligence reports that the opponent is preparing the decisive attack on Berlin.

2. The Heeresgruppe *must temporarily postpone* 'Angriffsgedanken' *and take all measures to support the front of the 9.* Armee *from the Stettin bridgehead."*

A noteworthy report! The "temporary postponement of '*Angriffsgedanken*'" displays how unreal the situation then was apparently seen in German staffs at this time. Originally Hitler wanted to advance from the Altdamm bridgehead toward Danzig (today Gdańsk in Poland)!

On 16 March 1945 the commander of the *SS-Panzer-Regiment* 10, *SS-Obersturmbannführer* Paetsch, fell during heavy barrage fire. *SS-Sturmbannführer* Tetsch took over the remainder of the regiment.

On 17 March 1945 things happened very quickly. The *Heeresgruppe* "Weichsel" reported again and again:

"South of Altdamm there is intense fighting at the rail line. At the northeastern front the enemy repulsed our own units in numerous positions 2 km northeast of Altdamm."

and:

"The enemy has invaded on both sides of the Reichsstraße *104 through the train station in Altdamm. Street fighting in Altdamm. The danger exists that the small groups of the Division 'Nordland' situated north of Altdamm will be cut off. The* Heeresgruppe *requests that this fact be discussed at headquarters."*

Hitler reacted before it was too late. The *Heeresgruppe* "Weichsel" was able to announce to the 3. *Panzer-Armee*:

"1. On the night of 19/3 Hitler has authorized the evacuation of the Stettin bridgehead.
2. Pz.-AOK 3 must execute the retreat from the bridgehead in order to ensure the return of all heavy equipment, primarily tanks, artillery, and Flak.
3. With the troops becoming available, defense of the Oder at and on both sides of Stettin is to be established, and there is to be the reinforcement of the sector of the Oderkorps *and the Langenberg bridgehead."*

The last sections of the 10. *SS-Panzer-Division* "Frundsberg" subsequently retreated back to the Oder on the evening of 20 March 1945. A former member of the *SS-Panzer-Pionier-Bataillon* 10 recalls the weeks in March/April 1945:

"At the end of February 1945 the loading of the train to the Fürstenwalde region took place. Here a Russian bridgehead was to be taken out. Everything that was needed on our side was available. Shortly before the beginning of the attack the order was rescinded, and we arrived via rail at Stettin again on 2 or 3 March 1945. There was a lot of talk of sabotage. The company moved into barracks in Stettin. The way to Naugard led through Altdamm. The convoys of refugees had become even greater and hopeless. In Stettin tanks were entrenched. Gollnow was lost. At a street embankment not far from Gollnow mounted Wurfkörper *were stored. Under the leadership of our sarge, Lindau, the* Wurfkörper *were aimed at Gollnow and brought along the way. The effect was dreadful. At Rosengarten, the company under Baumgärtel was directed into prepared positions [trenches]. We had many losses. The* Kompanieführer *Baumgärtel was wounded by shrapnel in his thigh. The medic was unable to staunch the blood and Baumgärtel bled to death. We buried him at an archway in Rosengarten. SS-Untersturmführer Berger became the new* Kompanieführer. *At the end of March 1945 we came back to the Stettin barracks. We learned that Stettin had been declared a stronghold. Vast quantities of alcoholic beverages were stored in the provisions warehouse. We no longer needed the winter clothing with the nice weather. The truck was unloaded, and despite protest from the* Kammerbulle *was stocked with the best varieties of French cognacs. We spent Easter 1945 in Stettin. Via rail we headed again to the Finsterwalde region. Here we were replenished. The required strength of man and materiel was met again."*

Rail transport of the I. (Panther)/*SS-Panzer-Regiment* 10.

SS-Unterscharführer
Olsson

Panzer IV and *Zugführer*.

Lausitz 1945.

Repair of a *Sturmgeschütz*, and honoring of members of the *SS-Panzer-Regiment* 10.

Mission in Lusatia

No longer at the main front, the 10. *SS-Panzer-Division* "Frundsberg," located in the Stettin – Brunn – Braunsfelde region, received an order from the *Gegneralinspekteur der Panzertruppen*. According to this, there were no longer any differences between the *Panzer-Divisionen* and *Panzer-Grenadier-Divisionen*, but rather a uniform organization for both branches of service was to be established:[38]

"*With the issuance of the new organization* Pz. Div. *45 it is uniformly ordered to reorganize all* Panzer-Divisionen *and* Panzer-Grenadier-Divisionen *until 1 May 1945. With this the* Panzer-Division *equals the* Panzer-Grenadier-Division."

Two *Panzer-Grenadier-Regimenter* to each two—no longer motorized—battalions was planned, as well as a mobile *Kampfgruppe* from a mixed *Panzer-Regiment* (I. *Abteilung*: Panzer and II. *Abteilung*: armored *Panzer-Grenadier-Bataillon*) and a section of the *Panzer-Artillerie-Regiment*. The *Panzer-Division* was to have a total of the following at their disposal:

54 *Panzer*
22 *Jagdpanzer*
90 *Schützenpanzer*

With this, such a newly organized unit—likewise in a *Panzer-Abteilung*—had less strength than an earlier *Panzer-Grenadier-Division*, whose two *Panzer-Grenadier-Regimenter* had three battalions (one armored) at their disposal.

The *SS-Panzer-Division* reported the following numbers on 25 March 1945:

35 *Panzer* IV (IV (II./SS-Panzer-Regiment 10)
47 *Panzer* V (I./*SS-Panzer-Regiment* 10)
10 *Panzer* "Sherman" (5./*SS-Panzer-Regiment* 10)
12 *Panzerjäger* IV (I. / *SS-Panzerjäger-Abteilung* 10)
6 *Panzerjäger* V "Jagdpanther" (2./*SS-Panzerjäger-Abteilung* 10)
8 *Flak-Panzer* IV (3./*SS-Panzerjäger-Abteilung* 10)
4 *Berge-Panzer* V
16 *Panzerspähwagen*
138 *Schützenpanzerwagen*
1 *Panzer-Befehlswagen* III
2 *Panzer-Befehlswagen* IV
5 *Panzer-Befehlswagen* V
1 *Artillerie-Beobachtungspanzer* III

---

38 *Generalstab des Heeres*/Org. Abt. Nr. I/1600/45 g. Kdos. From 24 March 1945.

7 *Artillerie-Beobachtungspanzer* IV
21 light *Feldhaubitzen* (I. and II. *Abteilung*)
12 heavy *Feldhaubitzen* (III. *Abteilung*)
10 *Kanonen* 10 cm (IV. *Abteilung*)
10 Flak 8.8 cm
12 Flak 3.7 cm
27 Flak 2 cm
8 Flak 2 cm Vierling
4 Flak 2 cm Drilling
8 heavy Pak 7.5 cm
9 K.W.K. 7.5 cm

With 369 *Führer*, 2,570 *Unterführer*, and 12,028 *Mannschaften* (total 15,000 strength) the unit reached nearly a complete strength in comparison with earlier required numbers, and was very strong according to the new organization of a *Panzer-Division* in 1945. Regarding equipment, the following prominent differences were seen:

10. *SS-Panzer-Division* "Frundsberg"	*Panzer-Division* 1945
92 *Panzer*	54 *Panzer*
18 *Jagd-Panzer*	22 *Jagd-Panzer*
138 *Schützenpanzer*	90 *Schützenpanzer*
21 light *Feldhaubitzen*	14 light *Feldhaubitzen*[39]
12 heavy *Feldhaubitzen*	22 heavy *Feldhaubitzen*
10 *Kanonen* 10 cm	4 *Kanonen* 10 cm

This was noteworthy in several aspects. Hardly any other division on the eastern front had an approximate equipment at this time, and the old *SS-Panzer-Divisionen* situated in Hungary reported on 17 March 1945 only:

	Panzer IV	Panzer V	Panzer VI	*Sturmgeschütze*
1. *SS-Panzer-Division*:	14	14	9 (*unterst.*)	4
2. *SS-Panzer-Division*:	6	8		19
3. *SS-Panzer-Division*:	16	8	7	17
5. *SS-Panzer-Division*:	4	13		8

With this the 10. *SS-Panzer-Division* "Frundsberg" displayed a great strategic reserve, whose replacements, however, were limited by the lack of fuel. To provide mobile, operative reserves in the *Zug* for the defense of the anticipated Soviet major offensive between Seelow and Lauban, the 10. *SS-Panzer-Division* "Frundsberg" received the order on 27 March 1945 to transfer to the south. Initially ordered to the Fürstenwalde region,

---

39 The *Panzer-Artillerie-Regiment* of a *Panzer-Division* 1945 had the following organization:
I. *Abteilung* with two *Panzer-Haubitzen-Batterien* "Wespe" to each 6 light *Feldhaubitzen* and a *Panzerhaubitzen-Batterie* "Hummel" to 6 heavy *Feldhaubitzen*.
II. *Abteilung* with two batteries to each 4 light *Feldhaubitzen*.
III. *Abteilung* with a battery to 4 10 cm *Kanonen* and two batteries to 4 heavy *Feldhaubitzen* 15 cm.

a short time later the marching order to the *Heeresgruppe* "Mitte" to Niederschlesien followed. In the area between the 4. *Panzer-Armee* and the 17. Armee in the region east of Görlitz to south of Lauban (division's command post: Heidersdorf) the unit once again had the opportunity for replenishment.

The 4. *Panzer-Armee* (*General der Panzertruppen* Gräser[40]) was located on an approximately 120 km long front from south of Neuzelle at Guben to the region of Lauban, and on 12 April 1945 was organized into:

V. *Armee-Korps* (south of Neuzelle to Muskau) with
Kampfgruppe/35. *SS-Polizei-Grenadier-Division*
214. *Infanterie-Division*
Kampfgruppe/36. *Waffen-Grenadier-Division der SS*[41]
342. *Infanterie-Division*
275. *Infanterie-Division*
344. *Infanterie-Division*
Panzer-Korps "Großdeutschland" (Muskau to Penzig) with
Panzer-Verband "Bohmen"
545. *Infanterie-Division*
Division z. b. V. 615
Panzer-Grenadier-Division "Brandenburg"
LVII. *Panzer-Korps* (Penzig to Lauban)
72. *Infanterie-Division*
6. Infanterie-Division

At the disposal of the army in the rear region of the army north of Dresden was the *Korps-Gruppe* "Moser" (*General der Artillerie* Moser) in formation with the 193. *Infanterie-Division*, as well as the *Divisionen Nr.* 404 and 463. Furthermore, in mid-April 1945 the *Fallschirm-Panzer-Korps* "Hermann Göring" arrived in the Hoyerswerda – Bautzen region.

When the Red Army arrived for the last assault on 16 April 1945, the 1ˢᵗ Ukranian Front (Marshal Konjew) succeeded in breaking through the main front of the 4. *Panzer-Armee* at numerous locations. The Soviet 52ⁿᵈ Army hereby advanced from the Neiße (today Nysa in Poland) – Bridgehead Niesky toward Bautzen – Königswarte, the 5ᵗʰ Guards Army toward the south of Spremberg, and the 13ᵗʰ, the 3ʳᵈ Guards Army, and the 3ʳᵈ and 4ᵗʰ Guards Tank Army in the region between Forst and Spremberg.

The *Oberbefehlshaber* of the *Heeresgruppe* "Mitte," *Generalfeldmarschall* Schörner,[42] ordered on 17 April 1945 the supply of the *Führer-Begleit-Division* (*Generalmajor* Remer[43]),

---

40 See Appendix 7
41 Compare Michaelis, Rolf: Die SS-Sturmbrigade "Dirlewanger" – vom Warschauer Aufstand bis zum Kessel von Halbe, Berlin 2003
42 See Appendix 7

as well as both OKH Reserv—21. *Panzer-* and 10. *SS-Panzer-Division* "Frundsberg"—
from the 17. *Armee* to the battered *Panzer-Korps* "Großdeutschland" (*General der Panzertruppen* Jauer[44]) in the Bautzen region. *SS-Brigadeführer* and *Generalmajor der Waffen-SS* Harmel was only able to partly comply with the marching order because the fuel situation was catastrophic. The lack of fuel led to the disbandment of the division. While the majority of fighting units marched gradually to the Spremberg operational area (Division's command post: Roitz), which was ordered shortly afterwards, the *Nachschubtruppen* remained primarily at Bautzen.

The 21. *Panzer-Division* reinforced the German troops in the Cottbus region, while the 10. SS-*Panzer-Division*, together with the *Führer-Begleit-Division*, reinforced the units in the Spremberg region. Together with the supplied forces west of Görlitz the opportunity existed to hit the flanks of the advancing Soviet armies multiple times. In order to counter this the Soviet 3rd Guards Army received the order to annihilate the German units at Cottbus, and the Soviet 13th Army, together with the 5th Guards Army, the German divisions at Spremberg (including those at the Spree bridgehead).

On the evening of 18 April 1945 the Soviet tank and rifle units had crossed the Spree north and south of Spremberg in a wide front, and thereby disrupted the majority of the *Führer-Begleit-Division* and the 344. *Infanterie-Division*, as well as the 10. *SS-Panzer-Division* "Frundsberg" from contact with their left and right neighbors. In intense counterattacks supported by tanks and *Sturmgeschütze*, the units attempted to prevent the looming encirclement. The Soviet attempt to take Spremberg was unsuccessful. Not until the supply of further troops on the night of 19 April 1945 could sections of the 13. *Armee* reach Neu-Petershain and make contact with the troops of the 5. *Garde-Armee*. The Spremberg pocket was closed! After heavy street fighting Spremberg was captured by the enemy on the evening of 20 April 1945.

The same day Hitler ordered the 10. *SS-Panzer-Division* "Frundsberg," which was located in the north, and now combined as *Korpsgruppe* "Jolasse" (*Generalleutnant* Jolasse, Kdr. 344. *Infanterie-Division*) with two other German divisions, to hit the Soviet troops on their flank and make contact with Cottbus. Contrary to the explicit order, the three remaining *Divisionskommandeure* on their own authority decided on an escape to the west! A former member of the *SS-Panzer-Nachrichten-Abteilung* 10 recalls:

---

43 See Appendix 7
44 See Appendix 7

"On 20 April 1945 the Spremberg pocket was closed by the Soviets. We received a radio message from Berlin: Frundsberg dies or closes the gap! As a result, SS-Brigadeführer and Generalmajor der Waffen-SS Harmel stated: 'It won't die that fast!' The next day the escape from the pocket began in a motorized march. Four Flak on Selbstfahrlafetten supported the escape. On 22 April 1945, under heavy losses we pushed through the Russian main front at Neu-Petershain and gathered at a swampy meadow after the loss of most vehicles. On the night of 22 April 1945 a few stragglers gathered in a forested area and reached the main front the next day."

Because contact with the V. *Armee-Korps* between Cottbus and Forst could no longer be established, on 20 April 1945 the OKH ordered:[45]

"The V. Armee-Korps (left Flügelkorps of the Heeresgruppe 'Mitte') will be placed under the command of the Heeresgruppe 'Weichsel' with immediate effect. It must maintain its current position to secure the southern flank at the southern edges of the Spreewald with the enlistment of Volkssturm."

A former member of the *SS-Panzer-Pionier-Bataillon* 10 recalls the fighting in April 1945:

"Upbeat, we went to meet the enemy on 17 April 1945. Up until the street sign 'Cottbus 6.3 km' we advanced quickly. Then the tanks reported that fuel was running out. The Russians evaded us – and proceeded on the freeway toward the west. The Russian soldiers sat on Panje-Wagen in the straw with torn uniforms and worn shoes. Our eyes became watery when we determined who had hit us."

On 21/22 April 1945 the remainder of the three divisions encircled west of Spremberg escaped through Kausche – Geisendorf – Neu-Petershain toward Senftenberg from the Soviet pincer movement.

---

45 On this day according to the memoirs of Artur Axmann ("Das kann doch nicht das Ende sein") a delegation of the *10. SS-Panzer-Division* "Frundsberg" took park on the festivities for Hitler's birthday: *"On the afternoon of 20 April 1945 I found myself with our delegation in the garden of the* Reichskanzlei*. There a unit of the* Kurland-Armee *and the* SS-Division *"Frundsberg" arrived. Hitler appeared from the bunker with Dr. Goebbels, Heinrich Himmler, Albert Speer and Martin Bormann. Hermann Göring was not with them, bur rather previously with Hitler. I made a report to the Führer. He walked with me along the front of the delegation. He walked with a slight stoop and held his trembling hands clasped on his back. He delivered a short speech... It was astounding what kind of willpower and determination this man had. Everyone was under his spell, including myself."* With this delegation it concerned a bearer of the Knight's Cross – *SS-Obersturmführer* Bachmann (*Adjutant* I./ SS-Panzer-Regiment 10) as well as SS-Rottenführer Storch (6./SS-Panzer-Regiment 10) recently decorated with the German Cross in Gold. Both carried a donation collected from division for the winter relief and a deed of donation from *SS-Brigadeführer* and *Generalmajor der Waffen-SS* Harmel. At 10:00 hours the reception was in the *Reichskanzlei*, four hours later Hitler's welcoming and on the same evening the march back to the division.

The 10. *SS-Panzer-Division* "Frundsberg" achieved the breakthrough while the *Führer-Begleit-Division* formed the rearguard with the front toward the east. At the outbreak, which initialized the disbandment of the division, the I. (Panther)/*SS-Panzer-Regiment* 10 took over the spearhead with *Panzergrenadiere*. The II./*SS-Panzer-Regiment* 10 formed the rearguard, with sections of *the SS-Panzer-Artillerie-Regiment* 10 firing a direct shot. At Kausche there was once more heavy combat, with sections of the Soviet 117ᵗʰ Guards Rifle Division attacking from the north and the 9ᵗʰ Guards Airborne Division advancing from the south.

On the night of 23 April 1945 the remainder of the three divisions finally reached the *Reichsautobahn* from Dresden to Berlin in the Wormlage region. Through Döllingen the men marched into the area north of Radebeul (area of the *Fallschirm-Panzer-Korps* "Hermann Göring"), which at the same time served as the assembly area of the 10. *SS-Panzer-Division* "Frundsberg." Here the units staying in the Bautzen area due to lack of fuel also set out to march. A former member of the *SS-Panzer-Jäger-Abteilung* 10 recalls:

"From south of Cottbus we transferred to Roggosen to the eastern side of a large lake between Neuhausen and Spremberg, and were constantly pressed by Russian units without tanks here. An evasion to the west was not possible due to the lake. Costly fighting followed in the forests east and southeast of Spremberg in which most of the armored vehicles were lost—and not from enemy action, but rather unskilled maneuvering in the forests and lack of spare parts. It amounted to the heavy fighting east of Senftenberg on a main street as we unexpectedly encountered a strong Russian flank unit on Selbstfahrlafetten. *Enemy tanks and* Panzerabwehrkanonen *then appeared. At this time I was commander of a* Sturmgeschütz, *and in the region of Groß and Klein Partwitz put eight enemy tanks out of action, but was then put out of action by a Pak during the capture of a village and while escaping received a shot to the shoulder. Also, the last* Sturmgeschütze *of our* Gruppe *were put out of action here. The* Fußtruppen *that were with us – there may have been 400 men – were stuck in a cleared area from the strong flank unit and had terrible losses there. One spoke of 200 dead that together with the wounded could not be rescued. On the continued march – one could also call it escape – we avoided all cities and moved in the protection of the forest."*

SS-Brigadeführer and *Generalmajor der Waffen-SS* Harmel and the first *Generalstabsoffizier*, *SS-Obersturmbannführer* Stolley, made a report on 27 April 1945 to the *Oberbefehlshaber* of the 4. *Panzer-Armee*, *General der Panzertruppen* Graeser, on the fighting at Spremberg. The next day, due to the non-execution of Hitler's order to advance north from Spremberg toward the V. *Armee-Korps*, a discussion with the *Oberbefehlshaber* of the *Heeresgruppe* "Mitte," *Generalfeldmarschall* Schörner, was to follow. The non-execution of the order to attack in the flank of the Red Army led to the dismissal of the *SS-Brigadeführer* and *Generalmajor der* Waffen-SS from the command of the 10. *SS-Panzer-Division* "Frundsberg." *SS-Obersturmbannführer* Roestel (*Kdr. SS-Panzer-Jäger-Abteilung* 10) was assigned command of the *SS* unit.

Deployment of the 10. *SS-Panzer-Division* "Frundsberg"
16 April – 9 May 1945

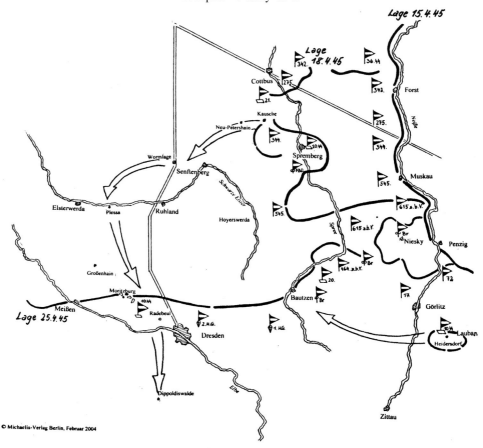

Last battles…

Last resting place…

A last mission took place for sections of the *SS-Panzer-Regiment* 10 and the *Panzer-Grenadiere* on 3 May 1945 at Moritzburg, north of Dresden. Two days later the remainder of the division marched in the general direction of retreat of the 4. *Panzer-Armee* through Grampitz – Dippoldiswalde to Teplitz-Schönau, which was reached on 8/9 May 1945.

A former member of the *SS-Panzer-Nachrichten-Abteilung* recalls:

"On 25 April 1945 the crossing over the Schwarze Elster at Elsterwerda and attack on Plessau took place. Through Bärwalde – Moritzburg in the region of Teplitz-Schönau, and on 8 May 1945 through the Erzgebirge to Leitmeritz to the SS-Nachrichten-Schule. *Because they set out for action, back again to Teplitz-Schönau and from there in small groups toward Komotau. On 11 and 12 May 1945 through the Grenzfluß at Joachimsthal to Klingenthal. On 31 May 1945 I was home again after an exhausting march on foot."*

A former member of the *SS-Panzer-Pionier-Bataillon* 10 recalls:

"After we had managed the breakthrough at Neu-Petersheim – Kausche, we found ourselves together across the way from Großenhain in Bad Schandau. A miserable remainder – but we had a few days of rest. The Stab *of our battalion was quartered in close proximity. The* Gerätewarte *and other servants had poisoned themselves with methyl alcohol. There were dead and blind people. At the beginning of May 1945 we drove with the remaining vehicles to Dresden into the* Pionier *barracks. Here files,* Wehrstammbücher, *etc. were being burned. On 6 or 7 May 1945 – everywhere white flags were hanging out of windows – we marched toward Prague. We went through Freital and Teplitz-Schönau until behind Aussig. Escapees and military approached us. We did not have contact with the enemy. Close to Aussig there must have been a concentration camp – the striped uniforms dominated. In a mountainous terrain a dispatch rider brought the news that war was over! Each person should try to reach the homeland. We gathered in a small forest settlement.* Untersturmführer *Berger said a few nice words, we cried, and headed west in small groups. All branches of the military and KL members with their striped clothing peacefully proceeded toward the homeland. At the crossroads Russians stood with captured BMWs and indicated the marching direction. Around evening we landed in a fenced-in camp. Here we would sleep and continue in the morning, the Russians told us. During the night most of the members of the* Waffen-SS *camping here decided to take off. We marched primarily during the night and stopped mostly in the forest. We evaded Teplitz-Schönau and finally arrived in Frauenstein.*

In Öderan we separated from the comrades who wanted to go to southern Germany. The remainder proceeded toward the west. The streets became more crowded again. From Flöha a proper re-emigration began. Those asked explained: 'The Americans are at the rear of the Mulde and are sorting out the members of the Waffen-SS *to have them fight for the Americans in Japan! (sic!)' How should they recognize us? We had ditched the tunic long ago. After we saw that soldiers with the Americans had their arms up with a naked upper body, and we learned that only the* Waffen-SS *had received the blood group tattoo, we turned around. We found places to sleep in a small village. The inhabitants were happy to have a couple of young men to protect from the encroachment of the victors. With razor blades we removed our blood group sign. We treated the wounds with healing earth. My ankle injury also improved. A few of us begged for potatoes so that we had something to eat. Others, including myself, tried to help at the local council. Straighten out evacuated schools and the like. Because we no longer had a pay book we received new identification cards from the 'old' head clerk. In mid-June I headed for home. On 24 June 1945 I, the former* SS-Unterscharführer, *was home again."*

Epilogue

With the surrender the division did not come into war captivity, like many other German units, but rather mainly broke up into smaller groups that independently tried to reach home. By doing so, the majority escaped Soviet imprisonment. Sections came into American captivity, from which most were released again in 1948.

In the 28 months of their existence the 10. *SS-Panzer-Division* "Frundsberg" had participated in numerous great battles of World War II. Beginning with fighting free the 1. *Panzer-Armee* in Galicia to heavy combat in Normandy and the defense of Operation Market Garden in the Arnhem – Nijmegen region, they carried out orders in the Linnich region as well as Alsace. Deployed to the front line in the Pomerania offensive, difficult battles followed in Lausitz, whereby the Spremberg pocket initiated the end of the *SS* unit.

According to the strategic utilization of a *Panzer-Division*, it was always assigned to the focal point of the operations. Because it was relieved by infantry units after the situation calmed and immediately deployed to a new region, the 10. *SS-Panzer-Division* "Frundsberg" usually remained for only a short time at a front sector.

Up to the fighting free of the 1. *Panzer-Armee* from the so-called Hube pocket in Galicia, great victories were denied to the division due to their localized successes. Nevertheless, they struggled with the given possibilities and situations with great motivation and effort until the end of the war against the numerically and materially superior opponents in the west and east.

Appendix

Appendix 1
Required Organization of a *Panzer-Division* 43

Divisionsstab
  Stabskompanie with *Kradmelder-Zug*
  Infanteriegeschütz-Zug
  Panzerabwehrkanonen-Zug
  Granatwerfertrupp
Feldgendarmerie-Zug
Army Post Office
2 *Panzer-Grenadier-Regimenter* to each 3 *battalions* á
  3 *Kompanien* with 18 1.M.G., 4 s.M.G., and 2 8.14 cm *Granatwerfer*
13. (*Inf. Gesch.*) *Kompanie* with 6 heavy *Infanteriegeschütze*
14. (*Panzerjäger*)*Kompanie* with 3 heavy Pak, 4 12 cm *Granatwerfer*
16. (*Pionier*) *Kompanie*
1 *Panzer-Regiment* with 2 detachments á 22 Panzerkampfwagen
  I. *Abt.* (*Panther*)
  II. *Abt.* (*Sturmgeschütze* or *Panzer* IV)
  Pionier-Kompanie
  Werkstatt-Kompanie
Panzerjäger-Abteilung with 3 *Kompanien* á 14 Pak on *Selbstfahrlafetten* (Sfl.)
Panzer-Aufklärungs-Abteilung
  1 *Panzer-Späh-Kompanie* with 4- and 8-*Rad-Spähwagen*
  3 *Aufklärungskompanien* with *Kradschützen* and *Volkswagen*
  1 heavy *Kompanie* with *Schützenpanzerwagen*
Panzer-Artillerie-Regiment with
  I. *Abteilung* á
  2 *Batterien* 10.5 cm *Haubitzen* (Sfl.) "Wespe"
  1 *Batterie* 15 cm *Haubitzen* (Sfl.) "Hummel"
  II. *Abteilung* á 3 *batteries* 10.5 cm *Haubitzen* (mot.)
  III. *Abteilung* á 3 *batteries* 15 cm *Haubitzen* (mot.)
Flak-Abteilung with 2 light and 2 heavy *Batterien*
Panzer-Pionier-Bataillon
  3 *Kompanien* (one on SPW)
  2 *Brücken-Kolonnen*
Panzer-Nachrichten-Abteilung
  1 *Fernsprech-Kompanie*
  1 *Funk-Kompanie*
  1 light *Nachrichten-Kolonne*
Sanitäts-Abteilung
Wirtschafts-Bataillon

Divisions-Nachschubtruppen
  1. *Kraftwagen-Kompanie*
  2. *Kraftwagen-Kompanie*
  3. *Kraftwagen-Kompanie*
  4. *Kraftwagen-Kompanie*
  5. *Kraftwagen-Kompanie*
  6. *Kraftwagen-Kolonne* (*Betriebsstoff*)
  7. *Kraftwagen-Kolonne* (*Betriebsstoff*)
  8. *große Kraftwagen-Kolonne*
  9. *große Kraftwagen-Kolonne*
  Gespann-Fahrkolonne
  Waffen-Werkstatt-Kompanie
  Nachschub-Kompanie
Feld-Ersatz-Bataillon with 5 *Kompanien*

Appendix 2
Military Postal Service Numbers

Divisionsstab	21 003
Feldgendarmerie-Zug	26 817
Military Post Office	26 310
SS-Panzer-Grenadier-Regiment 21	
Stab	27 001
I. *Btl.* (SPW)	25 685
II. *Btl.*	26 966
III. *Btl.*	28 227
12. (*Infanteriegeschütz*) *Kp.*	28 683
14. (*Fliegerabwehr*) *Kp.*	27 121
15. (*Kradschützen*) *Kp.*	29 562
16. (*Pionier*) *Kp.*	28 829
SS-Panzer-Grenadier-Regiment 22	
Stab	25 706
I. *Btl.*	29 638
II. *Btl.*	28 588
III. *Btl.*	28 383
13. (*Infanteriegeschütz*) *Kp.*	26 549
14. (*Fliegerabwehr*) *Kp.*	29 708
15. (*Kradschützen*) *Kp.*	27 274
16. (*Pionier*) *Kp.*	29 899

SS-Panzer-Regiment 10	
Stab	25 520
I. Abt. (Panther)	27 732
II. Abt. (Sturmgeschütze)	26 006
Pi. Kp.	26 427
Werkstatt-Kp.	28 113
SS-Panzerjäger-Abteilung 10	29 343
SS-Panzer-Aufklärungs-Abteilung 10	29 022
SS-Panzer-Artillerie-Regiment 10	
Stab	26 606
I. Abt.	27 311
II. Abt.	25 836
III. Abt.	22 513
SS-Flak-Abteilung 10	27 480
SS-Panzer-Pionier-Bataillon 10	28 028
SS-Panzer-Nachrichten-Abteilung 10	45 215
SS-Sanitäts-Abteilung 10	15 407
SS-Wirtschafts-Bataillon 10	27 654
SS-Divisions-Nachschubtruppen 10	
Stab	27 654
1. Kraftwagen-Kp.	26 751
2. Kraftwagen-Kp.	20 798
3. Kraftwagen-Kp.	29 205
4. Kraftwagen-Kp.	26 177
5. Kraftwagen-Kp.	28 499
6. Kraftwagen-Kol. (Betriebsstoff)	27 510
7. Kraftwagen-Kol. (Betriebsstoff)	23 363
8. große Kraftwagen-Kolonne	24 045
9. große Kraftwagen-Kolonne	20 905
Gespann-Fahrkolonne	28 499
Waffen-Werkstatt-Kompanie	27 908
Nachschub-Kompanie	25 161
SS-Feld-Ersatz-Bataillon 10	57 815

Appendix 3
Frundsberg Song

   Primarily in basic training the German soldiers had to rehearse various songs that
were sung during marching, among other things. In addition to general songs for the entire
branch of service (for example, the *Panzer-Lied* or the *Lied der Artilleristen*), there were
also unit songs. For the sake of completeness the Frundsberg song is documented here:

Drumming echoes through the land, war burns everywhere
heaven, hell, murder and fire, our sword gleams brightly,
Frundsberg Grenadiere, soldiers bold and proud,
have fierce hearts, are made of solid wood.
Up, over and through!
Fearlessly we trek through the night,
our songs are raw,
bloody were so many a battle,
but we remain victors,
Frundsberg Grenadiere, soldiers bold and proud,
have fierce hearts, are made of solid wood.
Up, over and through!
A game of dice, clinking of cups,
as well as drinking mates
a proper Landsknecht song
under black flags,
Frundsberg Grenadiere, soldiers bold and proud,
have fierce hearts, are made of solid wood.
Up, over and through!
Girl in the red poppy
do not be coy,
do you hear the trumpets sounding,
soon I must march.
Frundsberg Grenadiere, soldiers bold and proud,
have fierce hearts, are made of solid wood.
Up, over and through!
Frundsberg – you are our man,
it is your battle we are fighting.
Nothing can separate us from you
for you with risk everything!
Frundsberg Grenadiere, soldiers bold and proud,
have fierce hearts, are made of solid wood.
Up, over and through!

Appendix 4
Chronology

01-06/1943	Assembly in the Bordeaux-Limoges-La Rochelle region in the region of the 1. *Armee*
07/1943	Transfer to the region east of Biarritz
08-10/1943	Transfer to the region north of Marseille (19. *Armee*)
10-26/3/1944	Transfer to the Lisieux-Bernay region
4/4-25/4/1944	Mission in Galicia
26/4-11/6/1944	*Herresgruppenreserve* in the Rohatyn-Halicz region
12/6-28/6/1944	Transfer to France
29/6-1/8/1944	Mission in the Aunay-sur-Orne-Evrecy-Maltot region
1/8-5/8/1944	Mission in the Onderfontaine region
6/8/1944	Mission at Vire
7/8-12/8/1944	Mission at Domfront
13/8-21/8/1944	The retreat and escape from the Falaise pocket
22/8-7/9/1944	Mission of the *SS-Kampfgruppen* "Schultze" and "Paetsch," and march into the advised quarters area east of Arnhem
8/9-16/9/1944	Replenishment
17/9-18/11/1944	Mission of the *SS-Kampfgruppen* "Heinke," "Brinkmann," 10. *SS-Panzer-Division* "Frundsberg" and "Traupe" in the Neerpelt-Nijmegen-Arnhem region
19/11-06/12/1944	Mission in the region west of Linnich
7/12-5/1/1945	Mission in Upper Alsace
6/1-10/1/1945	Transfer to Stettin
16/1-24/2/1945	Mission during Operation "Sonnenwende" (Pomerania)
3/3-20/3/1945	Retreat from Stargard to Stettin-Altdamm
2/37-2/4/1945	Transport from Stettin to Görlitz
3/4-16/4/1945	OKH Reserve in the Görlitz-Lauban region
17/4-26/4/1945	Fighting in Lusatia
27/4-3/5/1945	Assembly of the Division in the Dresden region

Appendix 5
Bearers of High War Decorations

Knight's Cross to the Iron Cross
Astonishingly few for a *SS-Panzer-Division*, members of the 10. *SS-Division* "Frundsberg" were awarded with the Knight's Cross only eleven times, the Oak Leaves two times, and the Swords only once! In comparison, the 11. *SS-Panzer-Grenadier-Division* "Nordland" received 29 Knight's Crosses in practically the same time period of action. This could possibly be explained by the fact of the often-changing command. It is also interesting that no member of the *SS-Panzer-Grenadier-Regiments* 22 was awarded. The awards were distributed as follows:

SS-Panzer-Grenadier-Regiment 21	4 Knight's Crosses
SS-Panzer-Regiment 10	6 Knight's Crosses, 1 Oak Leaves
SS-Panzer-Aufklärungs-Abteilung 10	1 Knight's Cross
Div. Kdr. and *Div. Führer*	1 Knight's Cross, 1 Swords

SS-Obersturmführer Bachmann (*Adjutant* I./SS-Pz. Rgt. 10)	10/02/45
SS-Hauptsturmführer Bastian (*Führer* II./SS-Pz. Gren. Rgt. 21)	23/8/44
SS-Hauptsturmführer Euling (*Kdr.* IV./SS-Pz. Gren. Rgt. 21)	15/10/44
SS-Brigadeführer Harmel (*Kdr.* 10.SS-Pz. Div.) Swords	28/11/44
SS-Hauptsturmführer Keck (16./SS-Pz. Gren. Rgt. 21)	23/8/44
SS-Obersturmbannführer Paetsch (*Kdr.* SS-Pz. Rgt. 10)	23/8/44
dito. Oak Leaves	5/4/45
SS-Oberscharführer Rech (*Zugführer* 2./SS-Pz. Aufkl. Abt. 10)	23/8/44
SS-Sturmbannführer Reinhold (*Kdr.* II./SS-Pz. Rgt. 10)	16/10/44
SS-Untersturmführer Reiter (*Fhr.* Stabskp./SS-Pz. Gren. Rgt. 21)	23/8/44
SS-Obersturmführer Riedl (*Chef* 7./SS-Pz. Rgt. 10)	28/3/45
SS-Obersturmbannführer Roestel (*Führer* 10. SS-Pz. Div.)	28/3/45
SS-Obersturmführer Scherzer (*Führer* I./SS-Pz. Rgt. 10)	28/3/45
SS-Sturmbannführer Tetsch, (*Kommandeur* I./SS-Pz. Rgt. 10)	28/3/45

Honor Roll Clasp

Fahnenjunker Gebhardt (*I./SS-Pz. Rgt.* 10)	8/3/45
SS-Untersturmführer Hummelberger (*Führer* 6./*SS-Pz. Gren. Rgt.* 21)	27/6/44
SS-Hauptscharführer Küffner (*Zugführer* 2./*SS-Pz. Aufkl. Abt.* 10)	25/8/44

German Cross in Gold
The German Cross in Gold, which was conferred 19 times, was also not presented to any members of the *SS-Panzer-Grenadier-Regiment* 22 (sic!).

SS-Untersturmführer Baumgärtl (*Führer/SS-Pz. Pio. Bt.* 10)	30/12/44
SS-Obersturmführer Behrens (*Führer* I./*SS-Pz. Art. Rgt.* 10)	14/11/44
SS-Oberscharführer Ehrhardt (*Zugführer* 6./*SS-Pz. Rgt.* 10)	17/9/44
SS-Obersturmführer Ellwanger (*Chef* 4./*SS-Flak-Abt.* 10)	19/8/44
SS-Obersturmbannführer Dr. Günther (*Divisionsarzt*)	18/12/44
SS-Hauptscharführer Haas (*SS-Div. Begl. Kp.* 10)	25/8/44
SS-Obersturmführer Harmstorf (*Führer* 2./*SS-Pz. Aufkl. Abt.* 10)	27/10/44
SS-Obersturmführer Hinze (*Chef* 3./*SS-Pz. Aufkl. Abt.* 10)	19/8/44
SS-Sturmbannführer Jobst (*Kommandeur* I./*SS-Pz. Art. Rgt.* 10)	19/8/44
SS-Oberscharführer Kellermann (*Zugführer* 5./*SS-Pz. Rgt.* 10)	17/9/44
SS-Sturmbannführer Laubscheer (*Kdr. SS-Pz. Gren. Rgt.* 21)	20/1/45
SS-Obersturmführer Pühringer (*Chef* 2./*SS-Flak-Abt.* 10)	19/8/44
SS-Sturmbannführer Reinhold (*Kommandeur SS-Pz. Rgt.* 10)	17/9/44
SS-Obersturmführer Riedel (*Führer* 7./*SS-Pz. Rgt.* 10)	19/8/44
SS-Hauptsturmführer Richter (*Führer* II../*SS-Pz. Gren. Rgt.* 21)	14/11/44
Oberfeldwebel Spillner (*Kampfgruppe* "Knaust")	23/11/44
SS-Sturmbannführer Stolley (1. *Generalstabsoffizier*)	30/3/45
SS-Rottenführer Storch (6./*SS-Pz. Rgt.* 10)	30/3/45
SS-Hauptscharführer Thomas (*Zugführer* 3./*SS-Pz. Aufkl. Abt.* 10)	17/9/44

German Cross in Silver

SS-Sturmbannführer Rösch (2. *Generalstabsoffizier*)	18/4/45
SS-Sturmbannführer Schill (*Divisions-Intendant*)	24/11/44

Approximately 2,500 ethnic Germans from Hungary joined the *SS-Division* "Frundsberg" in 1943.

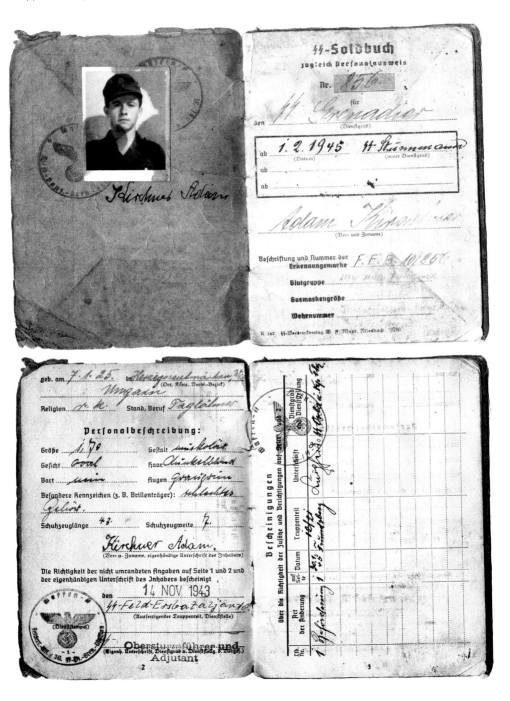

Appendix 6
Ethnic Germans in the Division

In contrast to the *Gebirgs-Division*, *Kavallerie-Division*, or the *Grenadier-Divisionen* of the *Waffen-SS*, which were largely formed of ethnic Germans from the southeast region, the number of these German expatriates in the motorized *SS* units that were formed at the beginning of 1943 was initially minimal. The 9. and 10. *SS-Panzer-Division* was formed from volunteers from the *Reichsarbeitsdienst*, the 11. *SS-Freiwilligen-Panzer-Grenadier-Division* from Scandinavian volunteers, and the 12. *SS-Panzer-Division* from volunteers of the *Hitlerjugend*. In these four motorized *SS* units there was a difference in the 11. *SS-Division*, because the anticipated quota of those reporting from Denmark, Norway, and Sweden reached only approximately 10% of the strength. *Reichsdeutsche* formed approximately 30%, while the remainder consisted of ethnic Germans from Romania.

The percentage of ethnic Germans—primarily from Hungary and Romania—in the other three *SS* units that were formed within the same time frame amounted to only 10%. Many from these were first conscripted to the *Waffen-SS* in late summer 1944.

The "advertisements" in Romania and Hungary differed temporally—together they had the goal that approximately 10% of the ethnic Germans would be conscripted to the *Waffen-SS*.

Romania

Aside from the more or less great actions[46] with which Romanian Germans were taken into German military service in 1940/41, the majority of the ethnic German conscripts initially served in the Romanian Army. However, a change was looming when, during the Stalingrad catastrophe, thousands of ethnic German soldiers left their Romanian units and sought admission into German units. This led to a harsh note to the OKW from the Romanian general staff in which "desertion" was discussed. The reasons for the abandonment of the Romanian troops was primarily due to their poor treatment. In addition to the obligatory physical punishment (beatings), with which generally all lower ranks met, the ethnic Germans were still deemed as "German *Hitleristen*," and experienced numerous disadvantages. The German leadership, which was now greatly interested due to the unreliability of the Romanian troops in bringing the ethnic German "Deserteure" in German formations, rejected the restitution of the men into the Romanian army.

---

46   The first came to Germany in the so-called "Tausend-Mann-Aktion" on 17 June 1940 and formed the III. *Bataillon der SS-Totenkopf Standarte* 12 in Prague-Rusin. In October 1940 the battalion transferred to Krakow and was incorporated into the 10. *SS-Totenkopf-Standarte*. With this, this was the first closed battalion of ethnic Germans within the *Waffen-SS*.

The *Oberkommando* of the *Wehrmacht*, the *Auswärtiges Amt*, and the *Reichsführer-SS* (*SS-Hauptamt und Volksdeutsche Mittelstelle*[47]) even went a step further and demanded the release of the ethnic Germans to German military service. On 12 May 1943 Hitler reached a compromise with the Romanian Marshal Antonescu on an "*international agreement on the classification of Romanian citizens of German ethnicity into the German* Wehrmacht (Waffen-SS)." Hitler's announcement to resettle approximately 537,000 ethnic Germans from Romania after the war had an impact that is not to be underestimated.

The advertisement ran across the German *Volksgruppenführung* in Romania, and the conscription followed through die Romanian branch office of the *SS-Ergänzungsamt* of Vienna. Although the majority of those fit for military service voluntarily reported, there was also pressure. The head of the *SS-Hauptamt*, *SS-Obergruppenführer* and *General der Waffen-SS* Gottlob Berger, once expressed:

"*Whenever a* Volksgruppe *is led halfway reasonably, then everyone reports voluntarily and those who do not report voluntarily have their houses battered. There were such instances in Romanian Banat within the last days.*"

Already as of 20 May 1943 there were transports every day through Vienna to Germany. The *Waffen-SS* had planned on 20,000 to 30,000 men, but the result was double. Up to 28 December 1943 43,000 ethnic Germans from Romania were incorporated into the *Waffen-SS*. Until the occupation of Romania by the Red Army in August 1944 a further mobilization wave followed. Of the roughly 70,000 ethnic Germans from Romania who were incorporated into the *Waffen-SS*, approximately 1,500 came through Vienna in October 1944 to the 10. *SS-Panzer-Division* "Frundsberg."

---

47 The *Volksdeutsche Mittelstelle* was established in 1936 for the administration of all financial means for the ethnic Germans and was initially under the "*Stellvertreter des Führers*." Placed under the SS on 1 January 1937, *SS-Obergruppenführer* Lorenz took over command. The *Volksdeutsche Mittelstelle* received additional tasks in 1939/40 with the settlement of Ethnic Germans from Poland and the Baltic countries. The numerous developing resettlement camps served, among other things, in the recruitment of Ethnic Germans fit for service to the *Waffen-SS*.

Hungary

On 6-9 January 1942 *Reichsaußenminister* von Rippentrop visited the Hungarian Prime Minister, Dr. v. Bárdossy, in Budapest for the release of Hungarian citizens of German descent for German military service (strength of the German ethnic group in Hungary approximately 1,250,000 people). After successful talks, from over 25,000 reports until summer 1942 approximately 17,000 able bodied could be conscripted into the *Waffen-SS*.

A second large mobilization wave was initiated at the end of August / beginning of September 1943, and was ended on 8 February 1944. On 28 December 1943 the number of ethnic Germans from Hungary gathered for the *Waffen-SS* amounted to approximately 22,000 men, who gradually reached Vienna. Here they were greeted by *SS-Obergruppenführer* Lorenz with a great production.

The option of voluntariness, which by the second conscription wave was only listed on paper, changed after the conclusion of the agreement between the German and Hungarian governments on 14 April 1944 into an absolute forced recruitment up until the age of 60! The signed agreement by *Generaloberst* v. Csatay (in the name of the Royal Hungarian Government) and Dr. Veesenmayer (in the name of the Government of the German Reich) led to the conscription of approximately 60,000 ethnic Germans!

Altogether, over 100,000 ethnic Germans from Hungary were conscripted into the German military service. From the approximately 80,000 men conscripted into the *Waffen-SS*, approximately 2,5000 (mostly in 1943) came to the 10. *SS-Panzer-Division* "Frundsberg."

Appendix 7
Biographies

Wilhelm Bittrich was born on 26 February 1894 in Wernigerode, and participated in the *Reserve-Jäger-Bataillon* 19, among others, in World War I. Having transferred to the Imperial Air Corps, in 1918 he belonged to the *Jagdstaffel* 37. After his membership to the *Freikorps* "Hülsen," entry into the *Reichswehr* followed in 1923. In 1930 Bittrich left active duty; however, on 15 July 1933 he joined *Schutzstaffel*, and on 25 August 1934 took over the II./*SS-Standarte* "Deutschland." On 19 October 1941, with the takeover of the *SS-Division* "Reich," he received promotion to *SS-Brigadeführer* and *Generalmajor der Waffen-SS*. In June 1942 Bittrich was assigned with the formation of the *SS-Kavallerie-Division*, and as of 11 February 1943 with the command of the *SS-Panzer-Grenadier-Division* "Hohenstaufen" (later the 9. *SS-Panzer-Division*). On 1 July 1944 he took over — as of 1 August 1944 — *SS-Obergruppenführer* and *General der Waffen-SS* – the II. *SS-Panzer-Korps* in Normandy. Bittrich, decorated with the Knight's Cross with Oak Leaves and Swords, died on 19 April 1979 in Wolfratshausen.

Kurt Chill was born on 1 May 1895 in Thorn, and on 1 April 1913 joined the *Infanterie-Regiment* 21 as a one-year volunteer. On 27 January 1915 he was *Leutnant* in the *Infanterie-Regiment* 61. After World War I he served in the *Schutzpolizei*, and on 1 October 1936 was brought into the army as Major. Initially commander of the I./*Infanterie-Regiment* 1, Chill (*Oberstleutnant* since 1 March 1938) became a tactical instructor at the *Heeres-Nachrichtenschule* on 1 February 1940. On 24 December 1940 he took over the *Infanterie-Regiment* 45. As *Oberst* (March 1, 1942) Chill led the 122. *Infanterie-Division*, and on 1 December 1942 received appointment to *Generalmajor*. Promoted to *Generalleutnant* on 1 June 1943, as of 1 February 1944 he commanded the 85. *Infanterie-Division*, and as of 5 February 1945 the LV. *Armee-Korps*. Chill was awarded the Knight's Cross of the Iron Cross.

Lothar Debes was born on 21 June 1890 in Eichstätt and joined the 18. *Bavarian Infanterie-Regiment* "Prinz Ludwig Ferdinand" as *Fähnrich*. Having moved into the Prussian Army, after completing *Kriegsschule* in Danzig he was appointed to *Leutnant* in the *Infanterie-Regiment* 88. In World War I he participated with the head of the *Feldeisenbahnwesen*, among other things, and with the rank of *Hauptmann* left military service in 1919. On 1 March 1937 with the rank of a *Sturmbannführer* he entered the *Waffen-SS* and served as a tactical instructor at the *SS-Junkerschule* Braunschweig. After the appointment to *SS-Obersturmbannführer* on 11 September 1938, on 1 January 1940 followed the promotion to *SS-Standartenführer* and command of the *SS-Junkerschule* Braunschweig. After the appointment to *SS-Oberführer* on 9 November 1940, as of 1 January 1942 followed the command of the 2. *SS-Infanterie-Brigade* (mot.). Next he led a *Kampfgruppe* on the Wolchow, primarily formed from *Wehrmacht* units as well as the *SS-Infanterie-Regiment* 9 (mot.). As of 21 June 1942 *SS-Brigadeführer* and *Generalmajor der Waffen-SS*, he commanded as of 1 August 1942 the *SS-Junkerschule* Tölz. From 15 January until 15 November 1943 he commanded the 10. *SS-Panzer-Grenadier-Division* "Karl der Große" (renamed and reorganized to the *SS-Panzer-Division* "Frundsberg" on 3 October 1943), and subsequently until the beginning of June 1944—*SS-Gruppenführer* and *Generalleutnant der Waffen-SS* since 30 January 1944—the 6. *SS-Gebirgs-Division* "Nord." From 15 June until 8 November 1944 he held the position of the *Höherer SS- und Polizeiführer* "Ost," and afterwards Debes served as commander of the *Waffen-SS* in Italy.

Karl Decker was born on November 30, 1897, in Borntin (Pomerania), and entered military service on August 3, 1914, as *Fahnenjunker*. On July 12, 1915, he obtained the rank of a *Leutnant* in the *Infanterie-Regiment* 54.

After World War I Decker served in the *Reichswehr*, and on 1 April 1939 was appointed *Oberstleutnant* in the *Wehrmacht*. Initially commander of the *Panzer-Abwehr-Abteilung* 38, on 10 April 1940 he took over the I./*Panzer-Regiment* 3 and on 15 May 1941 command of the entire Regiment. On 1 June 1943 he was assigned the command of the 21 *Panzer-Brigade*, and on 7 September 1943 with the command of the 5. *Panzer-Division* during which he obtained the rank of *Generalmajor* on 1 December 1943. After Decker was promoted to *Generalleutnant* on 1 June 1944, on 15 October of the same year he led the XXXIX. *Panzer-Korps*. Appointed to *General der Panzertruppen* on 1 January 1945 Decker, decorated with the Oak Leaves to the Knight's Cross of the Iron Cross, committed suicide at the end of the war.

Hanz Freiherr von Funck was born in Aachen on 23 December 1891, and entered military service in 1914. As *Oberst*, in 1939 he served as military attaché in Lisbon, and on 15 October 1939 took over the *Panzer-Regiment* 5. The command of the 3. *Panzer-Brigade* followed as of 13 November 1940, and after appointment to *Generalmajor* on 1 January 1941 the command of the 5. light *Division*. Already on 15 February 1941 he took over the 7. *Panzer-Division*. On 7 December 1942 *Generalleutnant* (1 September 1942) Funck became commanding General of the XXIII. *Armee-Korps*. With the promotion to *General der Panzertruppen* on 5 March 1944 he commanded the XXXXVII. *Panzer-Korps*. On 28 February 1945 Funck, awarded with the Oak Leaves to the Knight's Cross of the Iron Cross, was discharged from active duty.

Fritz-Hubert Graeser was born in Frankfurt/Oder on 3 November 1888, and on 28 February 1907 entered military service as *Kadett*. One year later he was appointed to *Leutnant* in the *Grenadier-Regiment* 12. Demobilized in 1920 after World War I, in October 1933 he entered the army again. As Major he commanded the *MG-Bataillon* 8 as of 1935. Promoted to *Oberstleutnant* on 1 April 1936 and to *Oberst* on 1 October 1938 in World War II Graeser led the *Infanterie-Regiment* 29 until his severe injury on 11 July 1941. On 1 October 1941 he received the appointment to *Generalmajor* and, concurrently appointed *Generalleutnant*, commanded the 3. *Panzer-Grenadier-Division* as of 1 March 1943. In July 1944 Graeser participated in a training course for commanding generals in Hirschberg, and as of 1 July 1944 led the XXIV. and, as of 5 August 1944, the XXXXVIII. *Panzer-Korps*. After the promotion to *General der Panzertruppen* on 1 September 1944, the General, decorated with the Oak Leaves to the Knight's Cross of the Iron Cross, took over the 4. *Panzer-Armee*.

Heinz Harmel was born on 29 June 1926 in Metz, and in 1926 joined the *Reichswehr* for a short time. After an apprenticeship and advanced training in the agricultural field, in 1932/33 he worked in voluntary labor service, and then with the *Chef AW* (*Ausbildungswesens*). On 2 October 1935, with the rank of *Oberscharführer*, he joined the *SS-Verfügungstruppe*

– *SS-Standarte* "Germania." As *SS-Untersturmführer*, in 1937 Harmel served in the II./ *SS-Standarte* "Deutschland." In this unit he was appointed to *SS-Obersturmführer* on 30 January 1938 and to *SS-Hauptsturmführer* on 30 January 1939. *SS-Sturmbannführer* since 20 April 1941, he led the II./*SS-Regiment* "Der Führer." On 5 December 1941 Harmel, *SS-Obersturmbannführer* since 19 June 1942, received command of the *SS-Regiment* "Deutschland." *SS-Standartenführer* since 20 April 1943, on 15 March 1944 he participated in a *Divisionsführer* training course that he had to prematurely discontinue because on 28 April 1944 he had taken over the 10. *SS-Panzer-Division* "Frundsberg." On 18 May 1944 he was appointed to *SS-Oberführer* and on 7 September 1944 to *SS-Brigadeführer* and *Generalmajor der Waffen-SS*. On 27 April 1945 Harmel was discharged from command of the 10. *SS-Panzer-Division* "Frundsberg" due to disobedience to the *Führer's* orders and was assigned the command of a *Kampfgruppe* from sections of the *SS-Junkerschule* Klagenfurt, as well as sections of the 7. and 24. *SS-Gebirgs-Division* in Italy. Harmel, awarded with the Knight's Cross with Oak Leaves and Swords, died on 2 September 2000 in Krefeld.

Paul Hausser was born on 7 October 1880 in Brandenburg, and joined the 7. *Westpreußische Infanterie-Regiment* Nr. 155 as *Fähnrich*. After completion of the *Kriegsakademie* he served—*Hauptmann* since 1 October 1913—on the general staff of the army. He participated in World War I as *Generalstabsoffizier*, and lastly *Armee-Oberkommando*. In 1919 assignment in the *Grenzschutz Ost* followed, and as Major in the *Reichsheer-Brigade* 5 in 1928 Hausser led the *Infanterie-Regiment* 10 as *Oberst*. Four years later he left the *Reichswehr* and joined the *Schutzstaffel* in November 1934 with the rank of an *SS-Standartenführer*. Here Hausser was involved in the erection of the *SS-Junkerschule* "Braunschweig," and was *Inspekteur* of the *SS-Verfügungstruppe*. As of 10 October 1939, as *SS-Gruppenführer* and *Generalleutnant der Waffen-SS* he formed the *SS-Verfügungs-Division* in the Protectorate of Bohemia and Moravia. Promoted to *SS-Obergruppenführer* and *General der Waffen-SS* on 1 October 1941, as of 28 May 1942 the command of the first *SS-Panzer-Korps* followed. From 27 June until 20 August 1944 Hauser, *SS-Oberstgruppenführer* and *Gegneraloberst der Waffen-SS* since 1 August 1944, led the 7. *Armee*. As of 23 January 1945 he took over the supreme command of the *Heeresgruppe* "Oberrhein," and finally of the *Heeresgruppe* "G." Hausser, awarded with the Knight's Cross with Oak Leaves and Swords, died on 21 December 1972.

Georg Jauer was born on 25 September 1896 in Lissen, and participated in World War I as of August 1914 as a war volunteer. In 1916 he received his *Leutnant's* patent and served in the *Reichswehr* after the war. As *Oberst* he worked in the *Heerespersonalamt*, and as of 5 March 1941 commanded the *Artillerie-Regiment* 29. On 15 March 1942 followed the command of the *Artillerie-Regiment* "Großdeutschland," and on 20 January 1943 the takeover of the 20. *Panzer-Grenadier-Division*. On 1 April 1943 Jauer was promoted to *Generalmajor*, and half a year later already to *Generalleutnant*. Jauer, on 15 March 1945 appointed to *General der Panzertruppen* and awarded with the Oak Leaves to the Knight's Cross of the Iron Cross, commanded the *Panzer-Korps* "Großdeutschland" as of 12 March 1944.

Georg Keppler was born on 7 May 1894 in Mainz, and joined the *Füsilier-Regiment* 73 "Generalfeldmarschall" Prinz Albrecht von Preußen" as *Fahnenjunker* on 28 February 1913. Appointed to *Leutnant* on 19 June 1914, Keppler, dismissed as *Oberleutnant* on 31 January 1920, was taken into the *Schutzpolizei* in Hannover. Transferred to the *Landespolizei* Thüringen in 1926, after a short time in the army he took over the I./SS-*Standarte I* "Deutschland" on 10 October 1935. Initially of the rank of a *SS-Sturmbannführer*, on 20 July 1937 followed the promotion to *SS-Obersturmbannführer*. As *SS-Standartenführer* Kepper was assigned with the formation of the *SS-Standarte* "Der Führer." Promoted to *SS-Oberführer* in May 1940, the appointment to *SS-Brigadeführer* and *Generalmajor der Waffen-SS* followed on 9 November 1940. In summer 1941 he was assigned with the command of the *SS-Totenkopf-Division*. *SS-Gruppenführer,* and *Generalleutnant der Waffen-SS* since 30 January 1942, he commanded as of March 1942 the *SS-Panzer-Grenadier-Division* "Das Reich." Fallen ill in February 1943, at the end of August 1943 he took over the official position of the commander of the *Waffen-SS* in Bohemia and Moravia. *SS-Obergruppenführer* and *General der Waffen-SS* since 21 June 1944, from 7 April until 26 July 1944 he was assigned in Hungary. On 15 August 1944 he was appointed to commanding General of the I. *SS-Panzer-Korps*, on 30 October 1944 to commanding General of the III. (Germanic) *SS-Panzer-Korps*, and on 8 February 1945 to commanding General of the XVIII. *SS-Armee-Korps*. Kepper, awarded with the Knight's Cross of the Iron Cross, died on 16 June 1966 in Hamburg.

Erich von Lewinski, named von Manstein, was born on 24 November 1887 in Berlin, and through adoption received the name Manstein. On March 6, 1906, he joined the 3. *Garde-Regiment zu Fuß* as *Fähnrich* and received there the *Leutnant*'s patent on 21 January 1907. He participated in World War I as *Regimentsadjutant, Ordonnanz-Offizier*, and I. *Generalstabsoffizer*, among others, in the 213. *Infanterie-Division*. In 1919 followed the assignment in *Grenzschutz Süd* (Breslau) and the acceptance into the *Reichswehr*. In February 1934 Manstein served as head of the *Stab des Wehrkreises* III in Berlin. In February 1938 he took over the 18. *Division*, and with the mobilization in 1939 became head of the *Generalstab der Heeresgruppe* "Süd." *Generalleutnant* since 1 April 1938, Manstein worked in the same capacity as of October 1939 in the *Heeresgruppe* "A." As of 1 February 1940 he commanded the XXXVII. *Armee-Korps*, and in March 1941 (*General der Infanterie* since June 1, 1940) the LVI. *Panzer-Korps*. In September of the same year Manstein received the supreme command of the 11. *Armee*. After he was promoted to *Generaloberst* on 7 March 1942 and to *Generalfeldmarschall* on 1 July 1942, on 22 November 1942 he took over the *Heeresgruppe* "Don," which was later renamed "Süd." Manstein, awarded with the Knight's Cross with Oak Leaves and Swords at the end of March 1944, was released from supreme command after differences with Hitler and did not receive any further assignment until the end of the war.

Walter Model was born on 24 January 1891 in Genthin, and entered military service as *Fahnenjunker* on 27 February 1909. On 22 August 1910 he was appointed to *Leutnant* in the *Infanterie-Regiment* 52. After participating in World War I and service in the *Reichswehr* Model, *Generalmajor* since 1 March 1938, became head of the *Generalstab des* IV. *Armee-Korps*. As of 25 October 1939 he was head of the *Generalstab der* 16. *Armee*, and on 13 November 1940 commanded the 3. *Panzer-Division*. At the concurrent promotion to *General der Panzertruppen*, as of 1 October 1941 Model led the XXXXI. *Panzer-Korps*. On 16 January 1942 followed the supreme command of the 9. *Armee*, and on 1 February the appointment to *Generaloberst*. On 9 January 1944 Model took over the *Heeresgruppe* "Nord" and was promoted to *Generalfeldmarschall* on 1 March 1944. The supreme command of the *Heeresgruppe* "Nordukraine" followed on 31 March 1944, and of the *Heeresgruppe* "B" in personal union as OB "West" on 28 June and 17 August 1944, respectively. Model, awarded with the German Cross in Gold and the Knight's Cross with Oak Leaves, Swords, and Diamonds, committed suicide in 1945 in the Ruhr Pocket.

Hans von Obstfeld was born on 6 September 1886 in Steinbach-Hallenberg and entered military service as *Fahnenjunker* on 17 March 1905. He received his *Leutnant*'s patent on August 18, 1906, in the *Infanterie-Regiment* 32. After World War I he served in the *Reichswehr* and, as *Generalmajor* since 1 January 1936, commanded the 28. *Division* as of 6 October 1936. After the promotion to *Generalleutnant* on 1 February 1938, the appointment to *General der Infanterie* followed on 1 June 1940 concurrently with the appointment to commanding General of the XXIX. *Armee-Korps*. From 25 August 1943 until 30 November 1944 Obstfelder led the LXXXVI. *Armee-Korps*, and afterwards the 1. *Armee*. As of 1 March 1945 the General, awarded with the Oak Leaves and Swords to the Knight's Cross of the Iron Cross, was *Oberbefehlshaber* of the 19. *Armee*.

Erhard Raus was born on 8 January 1889 in Wolframitz, and entered military service on 18 August 1909 as *Fähnrich*. On 1 September 1912 he was appointed *Leutnant* in the k. u. k. *Infanterie-Regiment* 1. After participating in World War I and service in the Austrian Armed Forces he joined the *Wehrmacht*. As *Oberst*, as of 15 July 1940 Raus commanded the *Schützen-Regiment* 4, and as of 15 March 1941 the 6. *Schützen-Brigade*. On 1 September of the same year Raus was promoted to *Generalmajor*, and on 23 November 1942 entrusted with the leadership of the 6. *Panzer-Division*. With the appointment to *Generalleutnant* on 1 January 1943, on 1 March of the same year he was assigned as commanding General of the XI. *Armee-Korps*. Already on 1 May 1943 Raus was appointed *General der Panzertruppen* and assigned with the command of the XXXXVII. *Panzer-Korps*. As of 1 November 1943 he led the 4. *Panzer-Armee*, and as of 1 May 1944 the 1. *Panzer-Armee*. Simultaneously with the appointment to *Generaloberst* on 15 August 1944 Raus took on supreme command of the 3. *Panzer-Armee*. Raus, conferred the Oak Leaves to the Knight's Cross of the Iron Cross, died in 1956 in Bad Gastein.

Hans Wolfgang Reinhard was born on 11 December 1888 in Hohenstein-Ernsttal, and entered military service on 30 March 1908 as *Fahnenjunker*. On 19 August 1909 he received his *Leutnant*'s patent in the *Infanterie-Regiment* 107. After World War I and time in the *Reichswehr*, Reinhard, *Oberst* as of 1 July 1934, commanded the *Infanterie-Regiment* 11 as of 1 April 1934. At the same time of his promotion to *Generalmajor*, as of 1 October 1937 he became commander of the *Luftgaus* IV. One year later Reinhard served as *Infanterie-Kommandeur* 26, and as of 24 November 1938 took over the 35. *Infanterie-Division*. Appointed to *Generalleutnant* on 1 October 1939, on 25 November 1940, as *General der Infanterie* (1 November 1940), he became commanding General of the LI. *Armee-Korps*, and as of 1 July 1942 commanding General of the LXXXVIII. *Armee-Korps*. At the end of the war he led the acting IV. *Armee-Korps*. Reinhard, awarded with the Knight's Cross to the Iron Cross, died in 1950 in Karlsruhe.

Otto-Ernst Remer was born on 18 August 1912 in Neubrandenburg, and entered military service as *Fahnenjunker* on 1 April 1933. Two years later he was *Leutnant* in the *Infanterie-Regiment* 4. As *Oberleutnant Kompaniechef* in the *Infanterie-Regiment* 89, the war assignment as head of the 13./*Infanterie-Regiment* 478 followed. Remer was appointed *Hauptmann* on 1 April 1941, and as of 1 February 1942 led the I./*Schützen-Regiment* 10. Already on 1 April 1942 he took over the IV./*Infanterie-Regiment* "Großdeutschland." As Major (1 January 1943) Remer commanded the *Wach-Bataillon* "Großdeutschland" in Berlin as of 1 May 1944, and for his mission was directly appointed to *Oberst* by Hitler during 20 July 1944. As of 1 August 1944 Remer commanded the *Führer-Begleit-Brigade*, from which the *Führer-Begleit-Division* emerged in 1945. Remer, decorated with the Oak Leaves to the Knight's Cross of the Iron Cross, died on 4 October 1997 in Marbella (Spain).

Ferdinand Schörner was born on 12 June 1892 in Munich, and as a one-year volunteer joined the Bavarian *Leib-Infanterie-Regiment* on 1 October 1911. Initially a *Reserveoffizier*, Schörner became an active officer on 26 December 1917. After World War I and service in the *Reichswehr* Schörner, *Oberstleutnant* as of 1 March 1937, commanded the *Gebirgsjäger-Regiment* 98 as of 1 October 1937.

Promoted to *Oberst* on 27 August 1939 and *Generalmajor* on 1 August 1940, as of 1 June 1940 Schörner led the 6. *Gebirgs-Division*. At the appointment to *Generalleutnant* on 15 January 1942 he took over the *Gebirgs-Korps* "Norwegen." Already appointed to *General der Gebirgstruppen* on 1 June of the same year, on 1 October 1943 Schörner commanded the XXXX. *Panzer-Korps* and then worked from 1 February until 1 March 1944 as head of the National Socialist *Führungsstab* of the army. Commanding the 17. *Armee* for a short period, on 1 April 1944 with the appointment to *Generaloberst* followed the supreme command of the *Heeresgruppe* "Südukraine." He also commanded the *Heeresgruppe* "Nord" (20 July 1944) and "Mitte" (18 January 1945). Promoted to *Generalfeldmarschall* on 8 April 1945, Schörner, awarded with the *Pour le mérite* as well as the Knight's Cross with Oak Leaves, Swords, and Diamonds, functioned as *Oberbefehlshaber* of the Army as of 30 April 1945.

Max Simon was born on 6 January 1899 in Breslau, and became *Berufsunteroffizier*. Dismissed after a 12 year term of service in 1929, he joined the *Schutzstaffel* in 1933, and on 9 November 1934 received the rank of an *SS-Untersturmführer*. Within the framework of the *SS-Totenkopf-Verbände* Simon alone was promoted four times in 1935, and as of 1 December 1935 led the 1. *SS-Totenkopf-Standarte* "Oberbayern" as *SS-Obersturmbannführer*. He was appointed *SS-Standartenführer* on 11 September 1938. Simon, *SS-Oberführer* since 1 September 1941, led the *Standarte*—incorporated to the *SS-Totenkopf-Division*—until 1943. *SS-Brigadeführer* and *Generalmajor der Waffen-SS* since 1 December 1942, as of 12 November 1943 he commanded the *SS-Panzer-Grenadier-Division* "Reichsführer-SS." On 20 April 1944 he was promoted to *SS-Gruppenführer* and *Generalleutnant der Waffen-SS*. On 16 November 1944, Simon took over the XIII. *SS-Armee-Korps* as commanding General. Accused in various war crimes trials after the war, Simon, awarded with the Oak Leaves to the Knight's Cross of the Iron Cross, died on 1 February 1961 in Lünen.

Karl von Treuenfeld was born on 31 March 1885 in Flensburg. He attended secondary school in Flensburg, and later the *Haupt-Kadettenanstalt* in Berlin-Lichterfeld. In 1903 he joined the 4. *Garde-Feldartillerie-Regiment* Potsdam as *Fahnenjunker* and was promoted to *Leutnant* one year later. In World War I he was assigned, among other things, with the securing of oil production in Romania, and was discharged from active military service in 1920 as Major. Until 1939 Treuenfeld was occupied in a private enterprise, and in April of the same year joined the SS with the rank of *Oberführer*. As of 2 December 1939 he was the inspector of the *SS-Junkerschulen*, and as *SS-Brigadeführer* since 9 November 1940 commanded the *SS-Brigade* (mot.) 2 from 24 April 1941 until 4 July 1941. Afterwards Treuenfeld was the commander of the *Waffen-SS* "Russland-Süd und Ukraine." In mid-November 1943 Treuenfeld, appointed to *SS-Gruppenführer* and *Generalleutnant der Waffen-SS* on 30 January 1944, took command of the 10. *SS-Panzer-Division*. The administrative man with the mentality of a village schoolteacher attempted to enforce, above all, the ideological components in the management of the division—strategically he failed. After the first assignment Treuenfeld was already relieved. On 22 April 1944 the 10. *SS-Panzer-Division* "Frundsberg" received a radio message from the commanding *General der* II. *SS-Panzer-Korps*, *SS-Obergruppenführer* and *General der Waffen-SS* Hausser:

> "*The* Reichsführer-SS *has released the commander of the 10.* SS-Panzer-Division *'Frundsberg,'* SS-Gruppenführer *von Treuenfeld from this position with express recognition of his efforts, as he needs him elsewhere for important tasks.* SS-Standartenführer *Harmel is assigned with the command of the division.*
>
> *After handing over his responsibilities* SS-Gruppenführer *von Treuenfeld is to report to the* Reichsführer-SS. *I give the* Gruppenführer *a special thanks and recognition for his continued work with training and instruction and for his personal mission in the last weeks of battle.*"

A euphemistic message! Himmler and Hausser recognized Treuenfeld's effort in the training of the recruits; however, he was unable to cope as a tactical superior. An *SS-Standartenführer* replaced an *SS-Gruppenführer* (sic!). Nevertheless, for lack of an alternative, with effect from 24 May 1944 Himmler assigned Treuenfeld to front command once more—of the VI. *SS-Freiwilligen-Armee-Korps* (Latvian). A decision of serious consequence! Von Treuenfeld, the convinced National Socialist, was completely overwhelmed with the military command of the corps, and due to his hesitant and indecisive behavior in critical moments during the Soviet summer offensive carried the German resistance from one fiasco into the next. He was already relieved ad hoc on 15 July 1944 and transferred to the *SS-Führungshauptamt*. The former commanding General finally worked there as *Inspekteur des Kraftfahrwesens*! He was also not meeting demands here: on 6 January 1945 his dismissal and transfer to the *Führerreserve der Waffen-SS* followed. No longer utilized, Treuenfeld died on 6 June 1946 in American war captivity in Allendorf at Wetzlar.

Appendix 8
Staffing

2/15/43-11/15/43	*SS-Brigadeführer* Debes
11/15/43-4/28/44	*SS-Brigadeführer* von Treuenfeld
4/28/44-4/28/45	*SS-Brigadeführer* Harmel
4/29/45-5/9/45	m.d.F.b.*SS-Obersturmbannführer* Roestel
SS-Panzer-Grenadier-Regiment 21	*SS-Obersturmbannführer* Kohlroser
	SS-Standartenführer Deisenhofer
	SS-Sturmbannführer Laubscheer
	SS-Obersturmbannführer Milius
	SS-Obersturmbannführer Zollhöfer
SS-Panzer-Grenadier-Regiment 22	*SS-Obersturmbannführer* Schützeck
	SS-Sturmbannführer Kleffner
	SS-Sturmbannführer Schultze
	SS-Obersturmbannführer Traupe
	SS-Sturmbannführer Jobst
SS-Panzer-Regiment 10	*SS-Sturmbannführer* Kleffner
	SS-Obersturmbannführer Paetsch
	SS-Sturmbannführer Tetsch
SS-Panzer-Artillerie-Regiment 10	*SS-Standartenführer* Sander
	SS-Sturmbannführer Sonnenstuhl
	SS-Sturmbannführer Haas
SS-Panzer-Aufklärungs-Abt. 10	*SS-Sturmbannführer* Brinkmann
SS-Panzer-Jäger-Abteilung 10	*SS-Obersturmbannführer* Roestel
SS-Panzer-Pionier-Bataillon 10	*SS-Hauptsturmführer* Tröbinger
	SS-Hauptsturmführer Brandt
SS-Panzer-Flak-Abteilung 10	*SS-Hauptsturmführer* Schrembs
SS-Panzer-Nachrichten-Abt. 10	*SS-Sturmbannführer* Kruft
	SS-Sturmbannführer Batzlehn
SS-Sanitäts-Abteilung 10	*SS-Oberführer* Dr. Rothardt
	SS-Obersturmbannführer Dr. Günther
SS-Wirtschafts-Bataillon 10	*SS-Sturmbannführer* Schill

Appendix 9
Ranks *Waffen-SS*/Army 1944

SS-Grenadier	*Grenadier*	*SS-Sturmmann*	*Gefreiter*
SS-Rottenführer	*Obergefreiter*	*SS-Unterscharführer*	*Unteroffizier*
SS-Scharführer	*Unterfeldwebel*	*SS-Oberscharführer*	*Feldwebel*
SS-Hauptscharführer	*Oberfeldwebel*	*SS-Untersturmführer*	*Leutnant*
SS-Obersturmführer	*Oberleutnant*	*SS-Hauptsturmführer*	*Hauptmann*
SS-Sturmbannführer	*Major*	*SS-Obersturmbannführer*	*Oberstleutnant*
SS-Standartenführer	*Oberst*	*SS-Oberführer*	No comparable rank
SS-Brigadeführer	*Generalmajor*	*SS-Gruppenführer*	*Generalleutnant*
SS-Obergruppenführer	*General*	*SS-Oberstgruppenführer*	*Generaloberst*

Appendix 10
Key

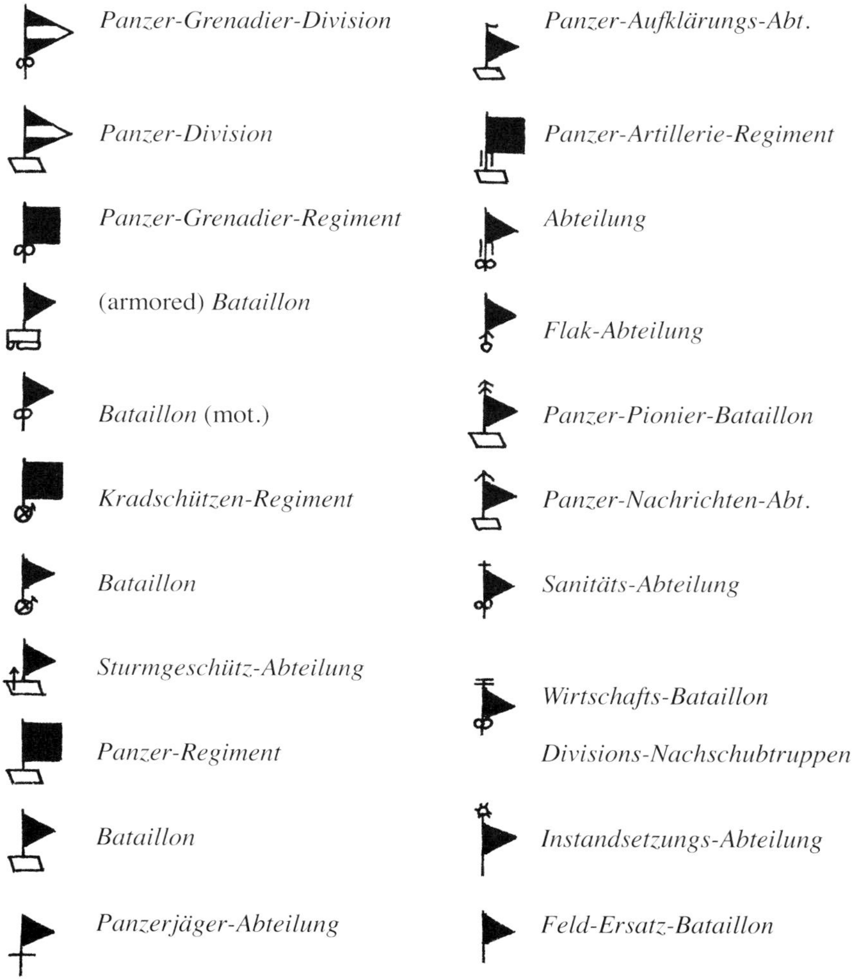

Panzer-Grenadier-Division

Panzer-Division

Panzer-Grenadier-Regiment

(armored) *Bataillon*

Bataillon (mot.)

Kradschützen-Regiment

Bataillon

Sturmgeschütz-Abteilung

Panzer-Regiment

Bataillon

Panzerjäger-Abteilung

Panzer-Aufklärungs-Abt.

Panzer-Artillerie-Regiment

Abteilung

Flak-Abteilung

Panzer-Pionier-Bataillon

Panzer-Nachrichten-Abt.

Sanitäts-Abteilung

Wirtschafts-Bataillon

Divisions-Nachschubtruppen

Instandsetzungs-Abteilung

Feld-Ersatz-Bataillon

Index of Names

Bibliography

Fürbringe, Herbert: 9. *SS-Panzer-Division "Hohenstaufen,"* o.O. 1984
Haupt, Werner: *Rückzug im Westen 1944*, Stuttgart 1978
Ders.: *1945 – das Ende im Osten*, Dorheim 1970
Hayn, Friedrich: *Die Invasion*, Heidelberg 1954
Hesse, Erich: *Der sowjetrussische Partisanenkrieg 1941-1944*, Göttingen 1993
Hinze, Rolf: *Letztes Aufgebot*, Meerbusch 1995
Kershaw, Robert: *Arnheim '44*, Stuttgart 2000
Klietmann, Dr. K.-G.: *Die Waffen-SS*, Osnabrück 1965
Ludewig, Joachim: *Der deutsche Rückzug aus Frankreich 1944*, Freiburg 1995
Manstein, Erich von: *Verlorene Siege*, München 1979
Mc Kee, Alexander: *Der Untergang der Heeresgruppe Rommel*, Stuttgart 1990
Michaelis, Rolf: *Die 11. SS-Freiw.-Panzer-Grenadier-Div. "Nordland,"* Berlin 2002
Otto, Alfred: *Die weißen Spiegel*, Bad Nauheimo. J.
Pilop, Max: *Die Befreiung der Lausitz*, Bautzen 1985
Preradovich, Nikolaus von: *Die Generale der Waffen-SS*, Berg 1985
Ritgen, Helmut: *Die Geschichte der Panzer-Lehr-Division*, Stuttgart 1979
Ders.: *Westfront 1944*, Stuttgart 1998
Scheibert, Horst: *Die Träger des Deutschen Kreuzes in Gold/Silber*, Friedberg o. J.
Ders.: *Panzer-Grenadier-Division Großdeutschland*, Dorheim 1970
Schramm, Percy (Hrsg.): *Kriegstagebuch des OKW 1940-45*, München 1982
Seemen von, Gerhard: *Die Ritterkreuzträger*, Friedberg 1976
Tieke, Wolfgang: *Im Feuersturm letzter Kriegsjahre*, Osnabrück 1975
Wagner, Carl: *Heeresgruppe Süd*, Bad Nauheim o. J.
Westerhoff, Bernhard, *Weg einer Panzer-Kompanie 1943-1945*, o. O. o. J.

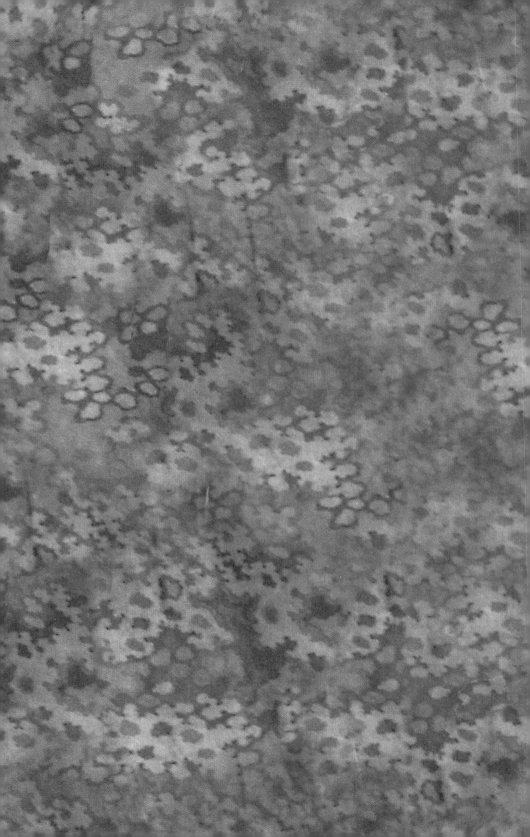